Building Lives
Constructing Rites and Passages

NEIL HARRIS

Yale University Press
New Haven and London

Published with assistance from the foundation established in memory of Philip Hamilton McMillan of the Class of 1894, Yale College.

Frontispiece: program cover, Chicago Day celebration and laying of cornerstone of the Federal Building, 1899. Illustration by J. L. Leyendecker.

Designed by Thomas Whitridge
Set in Scala type by Ink, Inc., New York, New York
Printed in the United States of America by BookCrafters, Inc., Chelsea, Michigan

Library of Congress Cataloging-in-Publication Data
Harris, Neil, 1938–
Building lives: constructing rites and passages/Neil Harris.
       p.   cm.
Includes bibliographical references and index.
ISBN 0-300-07045-4 (alk. paper)
1. Architecture and society—United States. 2. Architecture, American—History—19th century. 3. Architecture, American—History—20th century. 4. Rites and ceremonies—United States. 5. United States—Social life and customs. I. Title
NA2543.S6H37   1999   720—dc21   98-8100

A catalogue record for this book is available from the British Library.
The paper in this book meets the guidelines for permanence and durability of the Committee on Production Guidelines for Book Longevity of the Council on Library Resources.

10 9 8 7 6 5 4 3 2 1

To Teri with love

Contents

Acknowledgments

I AM GRATEFUL to many friends and colleagues for help and suggestions, but I want to single out just a few here. First, my thanks to the Buell Center for the History of Architecture at Columbia University, especially Gwendolyn Wright, for inviting me to give the lectures that are the basis for this book, and to Lew and Anne Davis for their hospitality during that visit. I began work on these essays while spending a wonderful year at the Getty Research Center, then in Santa Monica, where I benefited much from conversations with other fellows, notably Barbara Kirshenblatt-Gimblett and Joseph Rykwert. I did final revisions while enjoying another fellowship at the National Museum of American Art, Smithsonian Institution, and I am grateful to the staff and my fellow scholars there. Needless to say, librarians—at the Getty, the National Museum of American Art, and my home institution, the University of Chicago—were all immensely helpful. Graduate students Mike Wakeford and Laurel Spindel helped me check citations in the last stages of preparation. Finally, I owe completion of this text to my wife, Teri Edelstein, whose love, encouragement, and critical eye were all essential to the task.

Introduction

THIS BOOK HAD ITS ORIGINS in a set of three lectures commissioned by the Buell Center for the History of American Architecture at Columbia University. With some amplification and, I hope, some clarification, it retains much of the character of these lectures. In keeping with the mission of this newly created series, the presentations were essays in cultural history, exploratory statements negotiating between the highly specific realm of buildings as designed objects and the social universe that surrounds them. Their objective was to broaden historical perspectives on the built landscape by applying a series of analogies, taken from human experiences and from scholarly disciplines alike, to building histories.

anthropomorphizing buildings

The breadth of the subject treated here—spatial and temporal as well as conceptual—has been simultaneously exciting and intimidating. Indeed, its scale seems better suited to the informality of the lecture podium than to the printed page. Lecturers can be suggestive and qualifying; they can employ gestures, slides, and tone of voice to soften hard edges, indicate limits, raise questions, and multiply connections. Final decisions about argument and evidence can be postponed. But eventually, in stepping from podium to print, the gaps *and visually are, to everyone's dismay* must either be filled or bridged, decisions about what to include made final, and a much more limited number of illustrations selected for inclusion. Accepting the requirements of the book, and making these decisions, I tried to retain as much as possible of my original intent, which was to be suggestive rather than definitive about this *escape hatch!* large subject in order to provoke further research and reflection. And I have also tried to preserve the lecturer's sense of informality, of following up apparently unrelated details, much in the way that one might walk down roads simply for the sake of enjoying the scenery rather than in search of a specific goal. There are detours in the pages *another escape* that follow, maintained in the hope that readers will also enjoy some glimpses of unfamiliar territory, even if they are slightly delayed in reaching the promised end.

I have been encouraged in my task, if also sobered, by the fact that so little secondary literature has been devoted to the subject of this text: the building life cycle and its attendant rituals, occupations, and *Is it only in* representations. The absence of a paper trail can indicate either a *America that* remarkable opportunity or a misconstrued mission, one that mistakes *the bldg has* silence for meaning. I don't know why architectural historians have *a life cycle?* thus far paid so little attention to the rituals surrounding buildings, to their merchandising and graphic presentation, and to the creative responses that had to be devised for appropriate maintenance and repair. In a scholarly world where consumption culture, adaptive reuse, and the signifying other have achieved semicanonical status, such subjects should have been dealt with long ago. But with a few exceptions, they have not.

Buildings are among the largest, most expensive, and most permanent products of human labor. Their capacity to influence social and intellectual life, their role as status signifiers, their central part in the history of the world's religious and political institutions, their changing revelations of (and impact upon) domesticity, urbanity, and civic awareness are widely acknowledged. Yet beyond style and construction, the history of buildings as artistic subjects, real-estate ventures, and unavoidably aging entities with life stories that can be as revealing as individual biographies remains generally unwritten.

Thus I have been forced to make many guesses, basing them entirely on supposition or sometimes, when more fortunate, on fragmentary evidence. In order to provide a bit more coherence, I will concentrate upon the status of built structures in the post-Enlightenment world, and more particularly upon buildings in the United States. The reasons for examining modern structures should be apparent; the American focus results from my interests and experience. This does not relieve me of responsibility for tapping many kinds of literatures, and I remain concerned about omitting sources that are relevant. Even after admitting these constraints, though, I move with abandon across broad swaths of space and time, primarily to demonstrate the utility of the categories being applied. Such harvesting violates useful historical instincts and is not meant to say much about an enormous diversity of human societies. My primary concern remains with American society and its ritual performance over the past 150 years, but respecting these boundaries scrupulously proved to be impossible. I regret the errors and deficiencies that must result from any incomplete or inaccurate allusions.

The three essays that follow do not suggest architectural history in any conventional sense, nor are they framed as contributions to theory. I confess to the reader that I am fundamentally and unapologetically eclectic, humanistic, and traditional in my epistemological and phenomenological concerns. My interests lie ultimately in the construction of historical narrative. And my hope is that by naturalizing built structures, by subsuming them within a world that provides convenient models for this elaboration, we can learn more about their social and cultural role, particularly for structures that have commercial, religious, political, economic, or aesthetic significance within specific communities. Treating buildings as events, as occurrences, as subjects for biographical analysis is not meant in any way to deny their other roles. It is intended to supplement them. The quest for narrativity, which has become so animating a motive in many intellectual disciplines during the past few years, can find some satisfaction in the stories that buildings embody and, even more significantly, the stories that buildings ritually celebrate.

The sustaining assumption for what follows is a simple, not to say a simple-minded device. To see what might happen by treating buildings as if they formed some kind of special species, a hybrid class whose character, identity, survival, interaction with humans, and, above all, whose defined life stages merited systematic examination.

Of course this is a conceit. Viewed from any conventional angle, buildings are not a natural species. They are created objects that fit within no literal laws of growth; buildings cannot reproduce, act, evolve of themselves, fight, play, or do other things that animals do. Nor can they assume moral responsibility, speak, write, or perform in the manner of human beings. BUT...

I will not, moreover, in order to justify this strategy, take shelter within several long-established and carefully crafted linkages between natural organisms and architectural constructions. Thus I will not explore, except incidentally, the building as body, a prototype that has fascinated anthropomorphically inclined artists, architects, and critics for many centuries and which has invaded our nomenclature, literary criticism, and architectural allegories. Nor will I examine the building as natural object, modeled on or descended from trees, plants, caves, or other vegetable and mineral forms. This constitutes another influential source of legend and analysis. I am after something else.

Admitting that buildings are objects with their own special qualities and needs, what is gained by employing an animistic conceit? Is such a conception of the building collectivity as a species and of individual buildings as lives more than just a conceptual convenience? Probably not. But it is, nonetheless, deeply rooted and, as I will argue, embedded in the imagery popularly employed to describe buildings and the rituals developed to acknowledge and celebrate them. Few peoples have developed the comprehensive anthropomorphism of the Taberma, a Voltaic culture in Africa who conceive of their houses as humans and whose language and behavior reflect such convictions.[1] The Taberma greet their houses, feed them, eat and drink with them. But many civilizations, including our own, betray by rites and ceremonies a nagging sense that buildings constitute some kind of organic being, that they demand respect, attention, and care, for more than utilitarian reasons.

Occasional literary figures have developed parallel notions. In 1899 the American humorist Gelett Burgess prefaced his "Cycle of Modern Fairy Tales for City Children," *The Lively City O' Ligg*, by arguing for the intelligence of inanimate objects. "There was doubtless a stage in the progress of the two races," he observed, introducing his tales of talking, walking, and feeling houses, trains, and bicycles, "when animals and objects existed contemporaneously, and were equipped with approximately equal powers." "But the one was destined to go on and perfect a still higher culture," he concluded, with a bow to Darwin, "and the laws of Evolution triumphed. We can have no doubt but that it was a survival of the fittest."[2] This is not the approach taken here, of course, but it is reassuring to find the concept surfacing, even in lampooned form.

Studying buildings as a species also encourages, among other things, examination of certain key moments in the history of built structures. These are moments when, for economic, political, rhetorical, or ceremonial reasons, issues of purpose, style, scale, and expense are confronted and explored. That is, the conceit I employ here focuses attention on those occasions when builders, designers, clients, critics, publicists, and officials must talk explicitly about a building's larger meaning, when they are invited (or forced) to connect a structure's design, functions, and location with broader social concerns.

Such a conceit also brings into focus a whole range of occupations, practices, and instruments of expression that themselves depend on a building's life stages. I want to recover some of these moments, customs, and institutions in the interest of analyzing both their language and their logic. And that is why the metaphor of building lives seems so useful here.

Life studies have long fascinated commentators upon our own species. Anthropologists studying human rites of passage, those points of transition from one life phase to another, have illuminated priorities that change across time, exposing the varying emphases disparate cultures place on different life stages and the devices employed to signal their arrival. By applying this notion to buildings, by analyzing some forms of representation and ritualization, we may learn more about why we value some structures above others and how we indicate our continuing interest by adjusting to their needs and modifying our images of their personalities.

In these essays, then, I shall ask simple questions about how buildings are introduced and presented, maintained, celebrated, disposed of, and remembered. The subject in the first chapter is conception and birth; the next, growth and maturity; the last chapter will concern aging and death. The triple division seems to me persuasive. Whether it applies as universally to built structures as it does, across cultures, to human beings, is a matter still to be determined. But for better or worse, it is the pattern that has organized this book.

Joseph Pulitzer II laying cornerstone of
New York World building, 1889.

I

Meeting the World

ALL BUILDING is "necessarily an act against nature," writes Joseph Rykwert. "When you choose a site you set it apart from nature."[1] Throughout history such encroachments, in their many gradations and varieties, have called forth gestures of propitiation—ceremonies designed to appease angry gods, encourage good luck, and capture hidden sources of power.[2] In China, India, and Japan, as well as in Greece, Rome, and pre-Columbian America, the founding of cities and the planning of buildings were endowed with extravagant symbolic ambitions. Their location, their orientation to one another (as well as to the earth's directions and natural landmarks), the position of walls and streets were inspired by myths, surrounded with rituals, and celebrated by monuments and anniversary festivals. In the Roman world towns were purified enclosures; planners might consult the flight of birds, the motion of clouds, or the movement of stray animals to determine their precise sites and moments of establishment. Holes were dug into the ground to hold good things or contain the earth transported by the settlers from elsewhere. Secret naming ceremonies were common; the cutting of the furrows to mark town boundaries would be undertaken with a white cow and an ox, yoked together. The whole population participated in these public events, producing a common experience that was reinforced and made retrievable by means of the created landscape order itself—the pattern of its streets and the shape of its walls.[3]

The integrity of boundaries, the distinction between an inside and an outside, the orientation of rooms and furnishings have also concerned builders in many societies. Even today practitioners of feng shui, whose roots go back to magical beliefs, Taoism, and Buddhism, believe that the erection of shelters (along with other kinds of buildings) requires expert consultation in order to achieve harmony with their environment.[4] From Hong Kong to Manhattan, specialists are

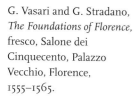

G. Vasari and G. Stradano,
The Foundations of Florence,
fresco, Salone dei
Cinquecento, Palazzo
Vecchio, Florence,
1555–1565.

hired to ensure that nature is not insulted by the shapes and layouts of structures.[5] Moving-in ceremonies, consecrations performed with the aid of chants and incense, are contemporary versions of rituals that thousands of years ago involved the sacrifices of animals or human beings.

Where everything is sacred, all buildings require special rites of consecration. In the modern American world of specialized landscapes, sacredness is most intimately linked with religious structures, and it may be appropriate to begin with them. As objects of presentation and inauguration these buildings have stimulated the most elaborate documentation, for they are simultaneously the best-studied and the most controversial sites for such rituals. Religious consecrations, depicted and referenced in various decorative schemes, have even affected the physical appearance of these buildings. "Dedication ceremonies . . . resonated in church art," writes Herbert Kessler.[6] In certain places, like Hagia Sophia for example, such representation perpetuated the consecration experience for all who subsequently entered the church, much as the design of ancient towns recalled their mythic origins. The mosaics of S. Prassede in Rome apparently depict the dedication of that church in 817, contemporaneous with

Justinian offering a model of the Hagia Sophia to the Virgin; detail, tenth-century mosaic, Hagia Sophia, Istanbul.

their creation.[7] In tile or paint or glass, the consecrating moment was preserved for future generations, an act of self-referencing that would expand to include other building types in later centuries, particularly courthouses, town halls, and capitols.[8]

Church and temple dedications mingled several things simultaneously: purification of the ground and the structure to make them receptive to sacred services; spatial division of the world into holy and profane; exorcism, if the building and its site had been used for pagan or heretical purposes; reaffirmation of faith and purpose; special heroic honor paid to patron saints; national and local demonstrations of pride; conspicuous consumption through expenditure on great scale and adornment; recognition of great donors; gestures of thanksgiving; opportunities for priests and lay people alike to exercise their special skills and reenact their social identities; and, perhaps most significant for some commentators, symbolic reenactment of the encounter between this world and the next, permitting, for the faithful, a foretaste of personal redemption.

Shrine of St. Taurinus, Cathedral of St. Taurin, Evreux, mid-thirteenth century.

Reliquary shaped like church; German, c. 1190.

Across the centuries bitter arguments contested the antiquity and specific lineage of these ceremonies for Christian churches, and furious debates erupted concerning their propriety and theological implications. Nineteenth-century Anglican traditionalists, for example, bent on relegitimating repudiated rituals, insisted that church dedication ceremonies had developed immediately upon the creation of Christian congregations. Some went even further. Every people who erected costly structures for a deity "thought it not enough barely to devote them to the sacred duties of religion, unless they also set them apart by some peculiar and solemn rite of a formal Consecration," the Reverend E. C. Harrington contended in 1844.[9] Harrington ransacked a broad range of sources, including writings of the church fathers and a series of commentaries, to support his position. Contemporary scholarship suggests, however, that before the fourth or fifth century the Church lacked specific and elaborate rites of church dedication; the first surviving rite is apparently sixth century, although relics were removed from earlier places of burial to churches as early as the fourth century. Earlier churches were considered to have been de facto dedicated by the solemn celebration of the sacrament of the Eucharist within the building, although older ceremonies included the consecration of the first or foundation stone. And although customary procedures had developed for bishops to dedicate churches in the time of Constantine, the elaboration of the ceremony awaited future events.

What helped change matters was the growing taste, in the Christian West, for relics. Persecution, civil war, and religious violence had produced a long series of saints and martyrs, and a Carolingian Church and state gave them a central cultural role as well as specific functions in oath-taking and church establishment. Pilgrimages, quests, and a lively, if illegal, international commerce, recently elaborated by Patrick Geary, generated treasures and relics.[10] These physical links to a worldwide church, and to history, were translated to Carolingian France and Anglo-Saxon England. Relics required special care and attention—and, among other things, special deposit in a church before the first mass could be said. A church acquired much of its sacral quality not from its association "with a distinctive site," argues one scholar, but rather through "its possession and sheltering of relics."[11] "Translations—the movement of relics to people—and not pilgrimages—the movement of people to relics—hold the center of the stage in late-antique and early-medieval piety," notes Peter Brown.[12] Without this experience the spiritual and physical landscape of Christianity could well have been very different, Brown suggests, perhaps more like the later experience

J. O. Davidson, launch of armored cruiser
Maine in the Brooklyn Navy Yard, *Harper's
Weekly,* vol. 34, November 20, 1890.

of Islam, with its permanently holy cities serving as the destination
points for pilgrimage.

It seems likely that the translation of relics directly stimulated the
development of highly formal ceremonies of church dedication. At
their heart, in the Roman Church, was the bishop's placing relics
within the cavity of an altar stone, which was then anointed and
sealed. Once this was done Mass could be celebrated and the church
consecrated. Elaborately decorated and constructed reliquaries and
shrines, magnificent enough to be venerated by the congregation,
became the proud containers of holy relics, on display for the faithful.

But church dedications were far more complex matters than this
simple procedure might suggest, even in the West, and varied greatly
according to the specific rite.[13] There were many analogies with other
objects, to be sure, such as the elaborate and self-conscious practices
associated with the laying of keels and the launching of newly built
ships and boats.[14] More direct ancestries can be found in the ceremonies associated with town founding in the ancient world, with
their heavy reliance upon divination as to time and place, hollowed-
out boundary monuments, and sacrifices. Anointing a stone filled
with relics symbolized the act of taking possession. But often the
bishop presided over a far more elaborate agenda when it came time

to dedicate a new church: after making three successive processions around the building, supported by his ecclesiastics and large crowds of lay people, he knocked three times with his staff of office on the door of the completed but empty church—empty save for a deacon who would open the door. As the door opened the congregation would literally take possession in the name of God.[15] If the builder of the church or chapel were a private individual, as opposed to an entire community, he would present the keys to the bishop upon his arrival, an inalienable conveyance of the property to God through God's representative, the church prelate.[16] It was crucial, according to some accounts, to have the transfer completed before any communion rite could take place in the newly established church. Processions within the church itself, sprinkling with special Gregorian holy water (a practice that held obvious baptismal implications), signing altars, tracing a great cross filled with an alphabet upon the pavement of the building, anointing twelve crosses affixed to the walls, these constituted a complex and richly symbolic service.[17]

Any aspect of church consecration might provoke immediate debate and sometimes even physical conflict. Thus the hour of the day or the day of the week for consecration was subject to discussion. In some parts of Europe this was limited to Sundays, but Pope Innocent III gave permission for churches to be dedicated on any day. Other popes approved dedication days to suit their ambitions and conceits.[18]

Embedded in these ancient ceremonies were notions of purpose and dominion; purpose was indicated not only by prayer service but by actual insertion of sacred objects, dominion by the transfer of the keys. And it was not only the churches as a whole that were specifically consecrated. Each individual altar, honoring a specific saint, required its own ceremonies. In the seventeenth century the bishop of Winchester, Lancelot Andrews, took to perambulating new churches, blessing every piece of furniture within them, and indeed every spot at which prayers might be offered.[19] Other prelates added their own personal touches, some bishops officiating, in rapid succession, over every possible form of service, from ordinations to burials, in order to inaugurate the space properly.

With their complex histories—building, burning, rebuilding, collapsing, enlarging, running out of funds, reconstructing, adding towers, altars, transepts—taking place over centuries, many ancient church structures were never completely finished. Indeed, the very concept of completing a building as of a specific date, delivering it, as it were, to the owners, all ready to go, is a modern notion. Celebrations of a great cathedral's final completion awaited the modern era. The 1880 ceremonies in Cologne typified the newer pattern. Earlier church dedications took place on a continuing basis, with no clear demarcations into absolute beginnings or first uses. And the consecration of a major church or cathedral was often linked to events other than completion of the entire physical fabric; much of the time, once the choir and a portion of the nave were enclosed and usable, the consecration date could be governed by political or military needs.[20]

The rich elaboration of consecration practices was rudely and abruptly checked in parts of Europe with the coming of the Reformation. The changes would have significant implications for Americans. Strenuously hostile to the veneration of saints and relics, and labeling many Roman Catholic rituals as superstitious nonsense, Protestants quickly tried to erase lingering marks of their older attachments. Catholics, after the Council of Trent, modified their own forms of worship.[21] Furious controversies erupted over altar and pew placement, the size and function of the rood screen, incense burning, stained glass, and the nature of the liturgy. Many reformers insisted that the physical church was simply a place of assembly, not a structure that required elaborate and mysterious rites of passage in order to become eligible for Christian worship. The presence of relics seemed unnecessary. Sixteenth-century Protestants defiantly held services in barns, in private homes, and in open fields as well as in churches. As part of their reform program, in England at least, early leaders banned ceremonies of church consecration, along with many other rituals associated with Catholicism. Acts of Parliament regulated the placement of communion tables and altars and even the permissible terminology.

Inevitably, these radical changes produced their own reactions. Even in the seventeenth century a long process of modification and softening began, as bishops and clergy within the Church of England sought to reestablish, albeit with modifications, many older procedures. But by this time the massive emigration to North America had begun, and many immigrants carried as part of their emotional baggage deep suspicion of any need to consecrate holy spaces as worship places.

The meeting houses that would become symbols of New England life and certainly the most important structures in the towns scattered across Massachusetts, Connecticut, Rhode Island, and New Hampshire were subjected to no significant introductory rituals. They were at first, like the town halls and meeting houses of contemporary England, multipurpose in character, sometimes little more than large houses.[22] For some years they hosted a variety of community activities besides church

Procession on completion of the cathedral
in Cologne, 1880.

services, including town meetings. At least 250 meeting houses were
built in New England during the seventeenth century, and over the next
150 years more than 3,000 additional churches and meeting houses
were erected in this region alone.[23]

Few records document elaborate services marking the inaugural of
these structures. And because there was no bishop in the American
colonies before the Revolution, certain kinds of ceremonies were
impossible, even for those denominations with more complex traditional practices. But if church dedications were simplified and constrained, it was common in the seventeenth and eighteenth centuries
for dozens, sometimes hundreds of neighbors to come together to
raise the meeting house frame, as they would in later years to raise
barns. These were occasions for feasting and celebration—gin, cider,
and rum provided as inducements to gain additional workers.
Sometimes neighbors threatened not to come unless such rewards
were promised.[24] The father of feminist Susan B. Anthony, a
Massachusetts Quaker, was celebrated for refusing to bribe these
workers with drink.[25] But with alcohol or not, the raising of a roof was
a major civic happening in the life of a town.

Old Ship Meetinghouse,
Hingham, Massachusetts,
1681.

But no specific ceremonies attended these events. Anglican, Dutch Reformed, Roman Catholic, Lutheran, Baptist, Presbyterian churches were also built in the colonies, along with synagogues—though no cathedrals. All these presumably were subject to specific religious customs at their dedications, but again, records are sparse and community involvement, beyond the congregations themselves, was usually modest.

Buildings began to achieve specialized purpose in the eighteenth century, but what changed everything even more dramatically was the American Revolution and the construction of a whole range of newly charged structures: legislatures, town halls, courthouses, executive mansions. These were not only prime examples of public ownership, they were soon perceived as opportunities for emphasizing communal identity. Both as objects and as investments, public buildings constituted affirmations of faith in the new constitutional system being created in America.

Even more significant was the coincidence of the new political order with the rise to national prominence of the Brotherhood of Freemasons.

Free masons

This fraternal association, whose roots can be traced back to the stone-mason guilds of the Middle Ages and, according to Masonic lore, much further back than that, grew emphatically, self-consciously, and aggressively in the early eighteenth century, first in England, then on the Continent and in North America.[26] The Masonic societies, though they claimed their origins in the building trades, were by that time dominated not by practicing masons but by speculative or accepted masons—that is, by merchants, artisans, professionals, and gentry attracted by the values and ideals the organization proclaimed. Such enthusiasm was stimulated by many impulses, among them anti-Catholicism, enthusiasm for the progressive social and political philosophy associated with the Enlightenment, love of nature, republicanism, a desire for fellowship, and the quest for a Biblically grounded, nonmonarchical ceremonialism, for rituals that expressed certain ethical principles but also preserved the excitement of secrecy and the drama of public theatre. The role of the Masons in the revolutionary ferment of the Western world has been much discussed by historians, who have variously found the lodges to be important nurseries of sociability and democratic self-government or breeding grounds of the Jacobin terror and the seeds of moralizing totalitarianism.

The links between Freemasonry and the new ideology of republicanism have been analyzed as both an intellectual and a stylistic force.[27] Less extensively explored is the emergence of their building ceremonialism, which, in America at least, owed a good deal both to the needs of the new nationalism and to the spirit of Masonry.[28] For at the heart of Masonic myth and legend stands the figure of Hiram, the builder of King Solomon's Temple, accompanied by a glorification of the principles of geometry and the secrets of building. Besides its appeals to benevolence, rationalism, fellowship, and history, Masonry encompassed a profound respect for the centrality and significance of the building arts.

American Masons confronted a remarkable opportunity. During the 150 years of continuous British settlement before the American Revolution, building rituals, as we have seen, were at best understated. For reasons dictated in part by poverty, in part by the dispersion of population, and in part by iconoclastic traditions, most buildings, Masonic halls excepted, were inaugurated in a casual and largely utilitarian manner. Royal and judicial etiquette dictated certain minimal ritual performances, but before the 1770s there were few great structures to celebrate and, in certain places, a religious bias against elaborate ceremonialism. What changed, opening up a new phase of republican ritualism, was elaboration of a political philosophy and development of political practices that were incorporative, integrating natural and built landscape alike into a cosmic and redemptive scheme of historical progress. The American republic became a grand stage in the evolution of humanity. Public buildings constructed in the interests of nationhood or meant to mark and monumentalize moments in the nation's history were naturally enough invested with special significance and dignity. But even private buildings bore evidence of a desire to share the reflected glory of the new society and to declare their fealty. Thus planning, completion, first uses, demanded ritual recognition and introduction as good republican operations.

But this was also a society that remained hostile—officially, at least—to the gorgeous pageantry, the manipulative pomp, the official splendor of existing monarchies. These rituals were seen as expensive and ultimately enslaving luxuries. The day was saved, in essence, by the presence of the Masons. With its comprehensive procedures, exotic regalia, complex system of historical referencing, and rich array of symbols, all in the cause of rational morality and democratic citizenship, Freemasonry offered a remarkable opportunity for matching lodge practices with the new social needs.[29] The Masons became the ritual mercenaries of the new republic, and the density of their architectural ceremonies was really quite remarkable.[30] Indeed, details of their procedures suggest the elaborate relic insertions that had now been associated with the Church for more than a thousand years and had an even longer history stretching back to ancient Babylon. Hostile critics attacked Masonry as a "gaudy show," and one of them, Cadwallader Colden of New York, a former Mason himself, found it extraordinary that in a republic country "where we claim to be such pure democrats" there "should be manifested in those who become masons, such a passion for finery, pageantry, dignities and titles."[31] This passion, however, engulfed many more than the Masons.

Thus a new era, probably a first era, began for American architectural ritualism in the 1780s and 1790s. The fact that so many heroes and military leaders of the Revolution, ranging from George Washington, Paul Revere, and Benjamin Franklin to Lafayette and Baron von Steuben, were Freemasons was still another reason to identify civic purpose with specific lodge rituals.[32] With astonishing ease Masons were able to dominate occasions of public dedication, etching their symbolic vocabulary onto the stone foundations of courthouses, battle monuments, city halls, and legislative chambers. In effect the sponsors and funders of these structures—either private members, congregants, and subscribers, for monuments and churches, or taxpayers and governmental bodies for the public buildings—turned over the ceremonial responsibilities for their initiation to lodge members. Some

William Williams, *George Washington as a Mason*, 1794. George Washington Masonic National Memorial, Alexandria, Va.

lodges proved especially active. In the second half of the nineteenth century Iowa's Grand Lodge laid cornerstones for almost one hundred buildings, including twenty courthouses and thirteen churches.[33] Freemasons became the most obvious instruments for building dedications.[34] It was not unusual for officials who were members themselves to don the aprons favored by the Freemasons and so emphasize their special level of participation.[35]

Of the various ceremonies of architectural introduction, the most significant, so far as Freemasons and republican Americans were concerned, involved the laying of the cornerstone. In later years and in some places, however, an earlier phase in the evolution of the building assumed some symbolic significance: the groundbreaking. Such events might involve nothing more impressive than shovels and spades, but as technology became more complex and machinery more elaborate, with enormous steam shovels to add touches of drama—and they were used first in the 1840s—groundbreakings could become quite dramatic.

Groundbreakings were also opportunities for low comedy and for

Boston Masonic apron by
Nathan Negus, 1817.
Museum of Our National
Heritage, photography by
John M. Miller.

developer publicity. As the construction of foundations became more
complex, long periods of time might separate the first spadeful of dirt
and the appearance of any superstructure. In the case of buildings that
were not yet fully paid for, the groundbreaking was a gesture of faith and
an opportunity for fund raising. It was a promissory note on a larger outcome, something suggesting a baby shower, held before the fact.

By contrast, the cornerstone laying, like a christening—or, for that
matter, a traditional cathedral dedication—represented a somewhat
more advanced life stage. The site had to have been prepared, the
foundations dug, the designs and dimensions approved. By the time
the cornerstone was laid, both appearance and financing were generally fixed. The cornerstone ceremony, then, became an opportunity to
introduce a broader public to a coming attraction, and it began a communal time clock, a means of measuring progress toward completion. Sometimes the clock was speeded up; when King Louis XV laid
the foundation stone in the mid-eighteenth century for the Church of
St. Genevieve, the church that would later become the Pantheon, the
royal occasion stimulated creation of a huge canvas-and-wood facade

Foundation-laying cornerstone for Cleopatra's Needle, New York, 1880.

Groundbreaking, Jones Laboratory, University of Chicago, 1928.

Benjamin Latrobe, *Masonic Procession for Laying the Cornerstone of the United States Capitol, September 18, 1793.* Grand Lodge of Virginia. Allen E. Roberts Masonic Library and Museum, Richmond, Va.

model to give participants a preview of the final result.[36]

The laying of first or cornerstones was described in the Bible and in even more ancient texts; such stones were present in the pyramids, and in the Middle Ages self-conscious ceremonialism surrounded the laying of the first stones for elaborate and expensive buildings like colleges, abbeys, and royal chapels. Like church dedications, first-stone ceremonies excited debates about timing. "Foundation stones were not laid lightly in the Renaissance," J. R. Hale noted wryly in his essay on the Fortezza da Basso in Florence. Astrologers, who had insisted that the building of the Palazzo Strozzi begin at 6 A.M., divided into different camps about the proper date for starting Duke Alessandro de Medici's fortress. After a series of negotiations and mediations it followed upon the bishop's saying of Mass in the early morning of July 15, 1534.[37] This, like other European foundation or first-stone ceremonies, featured extravagantly clad notables—church officials, noblemen, sheriffs, rectors, lord mayors, and, where possible, royalty—whose presence, in many ways, eclipsed the moment they were meant to celebrate. In the United States, on the other hand, the building, its functions, above all its communal presence remained the primary actor in the pageant.

Modern Masonic cornerstone-laying ceremonies are recorded in

Pierre-Antoine de Machy, *Louis XV Laying
the Foundation Stone of the Church of St.
Genevieve, Paris, September 6, 1764.* Musee
de la Ville de Paris, Musee Carnavalet, Paris.

England and Scotland during the eighteenth century, though they
were marked by a good deal of improvisation. In the United States
the rite was most extensively practiced and broadly understood during
the years between the American Revolution and the beginning of the
twentieth century.[38] It included, for Americans at least, an unusually
complex blend of ritual and symbolism. No detail seemed unimpor-
tant. Both the location of the cornerstone and the timing of the ceremony were significant. Ideally, although not invariably, the stone
would be placed in the northeast corner of the building. Masonic
belief made the north into a place of darkness, the east a source of
light. Placing the stone between them symbolized a progression from
ignorance to knowledge.[39]

The cornerstone itself, which could weigh several tons, was often
presented by the architect as a gift; it could be made of various kinds
of stone, but it was usually hollowed out to permit the insertion of a
metal box. Into the box, often of copper, would go a variety of documents and memorabilia fixing the moment and the place of the cornerstone laying: newspapers, the names of boards of trustees, direc-
tors, governmental officials, Masonic lodge officers, a Bible, the
Constitution, books, coins, stamps, currency, sermons, souvenirs, collected papers and speeches, building plans, bottles of whiskey (in the

Joseph Wencker, *Pose de la première pierre de la nouvelle Sorbonne*, 1885.

Arrangements for placing the first stone, New Sorbonne, Paris, 1885.

CAPITOL CORNERSTONE CEREMONY · 1793

Allyn Cox, *Capital Cornerstone Ceremony*, 1793. Collection of the U. S. Capitol.

Placing the cornerstone, the Bartholdi Statue of Liberty. Drawing by Schell and Hogan, *Harper's Weekly*, vol. 28, August 16, 1884.

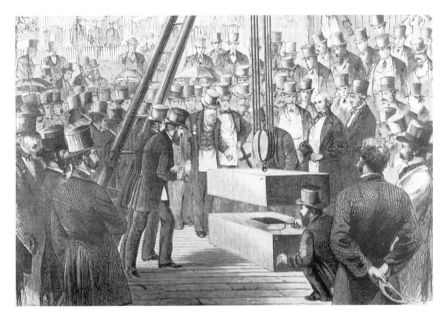

Laying the cornerstone of the new Masonic
temple, New York. Sketch by Stanley Fox,
Harper's Weekly, vol. 14, June 25, 1870.

case of at least one Texas courthouse), descriptions of the community
and lists of its leaders' names.[40] These were, in effect, anticipatory
time capsules of the sort that would be sunk with elaborate precau-
tions in the twentieth century to let future generations gain some
sense of what is considered to be our civilization.[41] Centuries earlier,
coins bearing the likeness of rulers had been thrown into building
foundations. By the nineteenth century the enclosure portion of the
cornerstone had come to reflect an acute awareness of the historicity
of built structures, their potential destruction, decay, or renovation,
moments of collapse that might yet preserve invaluable details for
successors. Things, in short, "that may be instructive and amusing to
remote posterity."[42] Or, as the mayor of Omaha declared in the 1890
ceremonies for his city's new city hall, "To its sealed recesses we
confide such evidence of our city's present size and prosperity as may
serve to interest the busy populace of some future generation, when
these firm walls shall have crumbled and the secrets of this corner
stone shall have been brought to light." The humdrum character of
the objects placed inside were signs of progress, for "from this recess
... will be taken no weapon of death, no evidence of barbaric wars, but
tokens only of peace and prosperity which have hitherto blessed this
city."[43] In an effort to document the actual moment itself, even copies

of the speeches delivered and the program of the cornerstone day's events were inserted into the enclosure.[44] Such acts captured the intense self-reflexivity that characterized these ceremonies.

Thus, when the United States Capitol was enlarged and a new cornerstone laid on July 4, 1851, Secretary of State Daniel Webster declared, as part of his oration, "If, therefore, it shall hereafter be the will of God that this structure shall fall from its base, that its foundation be upturned and this deposit brought to the eyes of men, be it known that on this day the Union of the United States of America stands firm; that their Constitution still exists unimpaired and with all its original usefulness and glory, growing every day stronger and stronger in the affections of the great body of the American people, and attracting more and more the admiration of the world."[45] Webster was speaking to his compatriots, just thirteen years before the Union actually, if temporarily, broke up. But his speech, which was itself deposited into the cornerstone, was intended, as he suggested, to instruct future generations about the present state of the nation.

The full history of cornerstone laying is yet to be written, but the assumption that the future would be absorbed by details of the past was one of its most significant features. It could be argued that in the new republic, relics had to be future-oriented; instead of the bones of saints, buildings would be built around the mundane desiderata of democratic citizens, of the sort described by the mayor of Omaha: their newspapers, their coins and currency, civic genealogies in the form of local histories, lists of office holders, records of committee meetings, the activities that foreign observers like Alexis de Tocqueville found, simultaneously, so novel and significant.

If this aspect of the ceremony was not specifically Masonic, many other things were. The procession to the cornerstone laying frequently involved the donning of special costumes associated with Masonry, most notably the ornamental aprons decorated with Masonic symbols and suggesting the occupational origins of the lodges; official lodge jewels were displayed, as well as swords, white rods, silver vessels filled with oil and wine, a golden vessel containing corn, and three major building tools: the square, the level, and the plumb. Ceremonial language, when the full Masonic ritual was presented, involved applying the tools to the stone, pronouncing it square, plumb, and level, and pouring upon it corn, wine, and oil, emblems of plenty, joy, and peace. The ceremony was concluded when the Grand Master or his stand-in gave three taps of the mallet to the stone. Other Masons on the scene would then clap their hands and alternately raise and extend their arms, folding them across their

Cornerstone laying,
Cathedral of St. John the
Divine, New York.
Drawing by T. de Thulstrup,
Harper's Weekly, vol. 37,
January 7, 1893.

Laying the cornerstone of
Central Building, New York
Public Library, 1902.

chests.[46] Often Masonic symbols were carved on the cornerstone
itself, or upon bronze tablets affixed to the stone or some other portion of the building. And accompanying this would be music,
speeches, and prayers.

   Not every cornerstone laying, even in the late eighteenth or nineteenth centuries, exploited the full range of Masonic ceremonies.
Indeed, a good many of these occasions were far less elaborate, adopt-
ing simpler and briefer programs and doing without the intervention
of Masonic officials. Sometimes, in the years after the Civil War, veter-
ans' organizations like the Grand Army of the Republic, which had
available their own suitable array of uniforms and medals, would dominate the proceedings. And congregations might or might not utilize
Masonic lodges for their cornerstone laying; purely religious formulas,
not so different in many respects from the Masonic procedures,
remained available. Thus, slightly more than one hundred years ago,

Title page for the
dedication services of
Isaiah Temple, Chicago,
1924.

Invitation to the opening of
a new building for the
Metropolitan Museum of
Art, 1894.

when the cornerstone of New York's Cathedral of St. John the Divine
was dedicated (with the participation of millionaires like J. P. Morgan
and Cornelius Vanderbilt), the presiding bishop employed liturgical
language, striking the stone with a special hammer when mentioning
each member of the Trinity, and smoothing the mortar with a silver
trowel while making the sign of the cross upon it.[47]

But whether religious, civil, or Masonic, the ceremony provided
an opportunity to affirm certain values and to associate the coming
structure with powerful natural symbols. In unlikely places, and
under improbable auspices, the cornerstone rite continued its
course. New buildings, like new people, were adventures awaiting
resolution. The need to wish the newcomer well, associate it with
hopes for long life and prosperity, and above all to dedicate it to the
performance of specific services made reliance upon symbolic marks
of goodness, bounty, and grace an integral part of the ceremony.
These connections were well understood in the Christian West. And

Procession and arch
erected to honor the donor
of the Peabody Institute.
Lithograph by J. H. Bufford,
1856.

as at christenings, everyone came dressed up. Official costumes and
silver trowels added to the sense of occasion. Selecting just the right
day—a patron saint's feast, a donor's birthday, an institutional
anniversary, a patriotic holiday—added to the sense of good fortune.
July 4, naturally enough, functioned perfectly for the cornerstone
laying of public buildings, while Decoration Day, May 30, served
almost equally well for other monuments. The feast, in June, of the
nativity of Saint John the Baptist, patron saint of the Masons, proved
an especially popular day for dedicating their own temples.

At other times, the presence of the donor inspired the ceremonies.
On October 9, 1856, the town of Danvers, Massachusetts, laid the cornerstone for its new Peabody Institute, the gift of philanthropist George
Peabody. The governor of the commonwealth, the president of Harvard,
scholars, educators, and politicians of importance were all present, and,
to mark the occasion, evergreen arches forty feet high were erected
along the parade route, along with illuminations, mottoes, portraits,
and mounted slogans.[48] These greeted a procession dominated by
marching school districts, each with its own float. The cavalcade of

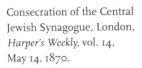

Consecration of the Central Jewish Synagogue, London, *Harper's Weekly*, vol. 14, May 14, 1870.

floats and carriages extended nearly half a mile, providing an escort for George Peabody and the other dignitaries. A special publication, lavishly illustrated, celebrated the event.

Introductory rituals did not end with the cornerstone laying, of course. Many years might stretch between the cornerstone and actual completion. The building, in this interval, was growing up, reaching maturity, not yet a functioning member of the larger community. Many cultures have occasions that signal the arrival of physical maturity and the acceptance of communal responsibilities. To celebrate such a status important buildings, aside from a groundbreaking and first-stone laying, featured a third opportunity for official presentation of self: their openings. This offered not only the chance to honor donors and supporters, to invoke history, to measure the progress made since the earlier ceremonies; it also encouraged, at a moment of maximal attention, definition and emphasis of purpose, a service of communion. Church consecrations, of course, had this at their center. But secular buildings frequently mimicked some of their details in the turning over of keys,

Inauguration of a Masonic hall.

for example, or the collective display of civic ceremony. If the structure
was a legislature or a courthouse, the governmental officials might
march in a body from their old home to their new. Prayers, music,
bunting decorations, speeches, and natural symbols, like plants and
flowers, were invariably part of civic and institutional openings in nineteenth-century America. Holidays were declared.[49] Special poetry and
music could be commissioned, or popular favorites performed. There
was a repertory, for example, deemed particularly appropriate to the
opening of concert halls and opera houses, Music To Begin Things
With: Beethoven's "Consecration of the House Overture" or the "Ode to
Joy" from his Ninth Symphony, portions of Mozart's *Magic Flute,* "Hail
Bright Abode" from *Tannhäuser,* or, as in the case of Chicago's
Auditorium Theatre in 1889, the simple singing (by the great soprano
Adelina Patti, in the presence of the president and vice president of the
United States) of "Home Sweet Home."[50]

One prevalent category of building opening that attracted widespread interest was the Masonic hall, built in large numbers across
the United States in the late nineteenth and early twentieth centuries.
The first building constructed in America for strictly Masonic purposes was erected in Philadelphia and dedicated June 24, 1755. In
attendance were Masons in full regalia, accompanied by the firing of
cannon and the pealing of bells. The ceremonies began with a service
at Christ Church and ended with a banquet in the new hall. In the

course of the next hundred years, as their numbers, wealth, and respectability grew, Philadelphia Masons dedicated ever larger and more costly halls, climaxed by the 1868 cornerstone laying and the 1873 dedication of America's most lavishly appointed and largest Masonic temple, a landmark for downtown Philadelphia. Into this cornerstone the Masons placed pieces of wood and marble believed to be taken from King Solomon's Temple, the physical inspiration for the building plan, along with more usual tokens of time and place. Thirteen thousand participated in the march celebrating the building's opening, and in subsequent days affiliated Masonic groups, including the Knights Templar, dedicated the building anew after providing citizens of the city with spectacular public processions.[51]

Another institution that accorded its dedication openings great seriousness was the public library, that secular church devoted to literacy, democratic citizenship, and economic mobility. Libraries, here and abroad, also of course enjoyed cornerstone and foundation-stone laying, but they commissioned especially formal celebrations when the buildings were ready for use. Programs could be quite elaborate and lengthy. Frequently library establishment represented a fusion of public and private support. And more than many other building types, libraries easily accommodated literary speechifying and references to education and learning. Schoolchildren, university students, teachers, public officials, patrons, and collectors—all could be involved with the opening ceremonies, which were repeated in such number that, like the buildings themselves, they seemed almost interchangeable.[52] The British opened their libraries with much of the same self-consciousness that Americans did and surpassed them in pageantry with elaborately costumed lord mayors and common councils. Moreover, British ceremonies were often graced by the presence of nobility, sometimes even members of the royal family.[53]

Secular building openings did not readily correspond with human ceremonies. While groundbreaking might be compared with the presentation of the newborn, and cornerstone laying with a baptism, the opening was a revelation of the mature object. Later on it could be enlarged, refinished, or renovated, but it was now complete in itself. The life cycle had moved on more rapidly than with a human being. The opening might better be compared with a debutante's presentation or perhaps a graduation. Invitations to opening ceremonies often proudly displayed representations of the completed structure.

While cornerstone layings, groundbreakings, and dedications were soon highly standardized building ceremonies, some of the most popular and best-covered nineteenth-century openings did not actually

Opening of the Hackney Central Library, 1908: awaiting
the arrival of the Prince and Princess of Wales.

Opening of the Central Library and Technical Institute,
West Ham, London, 1898.

Invitation to the opening
of Mandel Brothers
Department Store, Chicago,
1912.

inaugurate buildings. This group can be divided into two major categories. The first class consisted of presented objects that required a
public unwrapping. In the modern era, gift exchanges make unwrapping crucial to the sense of new ownership, and it is often—and
preferably—a witnessed act. Major industries developed to service gift
giving, and in some societies wrapping materials themselves—paper,
ribbons, boxes—have enjoyed special artistic status.[54]

Buildings themselves, at least before the era of Christo, were
impossible to wrap or unwrap. But they had some close linkages with
the unveilings of other large constructed objects, notably statues and
monuments. The literal origins of this custom are still not quite clear;
The Oxford English Dictionary proposes that the phrase *unveiling a
statue* was first used in the 1860s, which seems late. Long before then
statues were inaugurated with pomp and pageantry—but not, apparently, with the drama of the lifted veil. Once the practice was in place,
however, it grew almost universally popular. Unveiling became a
generic label for the larger ceremony of dedication, which was carefully recorded in the nineteenth and twentieth centuries through a

series of woodcuts, lithographs, and photographs, many of which were published by newspapers and magazines. Rarely was the design secret, for in many cases competitions had preceded the commission, and construction outdoors could not be easily hidden. But for dramatic purposes the statue, or as much of it as could physically be managed, would be covered, often just hours before being uncovered. This was a symbolic re-creation of the statue's birth and an emphasis upon its status as gift. Normally monuments in nineteenth-century America were not paid for by tax revenues but were financed by acts of individual philanthropy or through public subscription. They were invariably described as being presented by the contributors to the larger community—gestures of gratitude, loyalty, or benevolence.

Nineteenth-century Europe and America offered thousands, even tens of thousands of such occasions. Patriots, humanitarians, war heroes, monarchs, scientists, artists, millionaires shared honors with explorers, inventors, clerics, saints, not to mention the collective tributes to nationality, religion, republicanism, and the glorious dead. Obelisks, columns, arches, benches, fountains, plinths, towers, colonnades, as well as representations of people seated, standing, recumbent, astride horses, orating, pointing, and otherwise disporting, were numerous enough to constitute almost a new material universe. "The land is cluttered with stones that try ineffectually to lift leaden names out of the dust," complained one commentator.[55] No sooner did a celebrity die than campaigns were launched for a monument. "It is probable," observed a group of American architects, "that no important nation, perhaps none at all, has been so unlucky in its monuments as the United States."[56] Each of these tens of thousands enjoyed its own moment of introduction, orchestrated carefully by authorities and by groups of enthusiastic volunteers. Special holidays increased awareness and ensured crowds of celebrants, while parades, concerts, fireworks, and banquets completed these dedicatory festivals.[57]

Such occasions constituted obvious events for the growing journalistic community to cover; their descriptions emphasized the dramatic elements. A special breathlessness seemed to attend the narration of monument unveilings. From thousands of possibilities I cite the excited reaction of *Harper's Weekly* to the unveiling of sculptor Harriet Hosmer's rendition of the old Jacksonian political leader William Hart Benton. The great event took place in St. Louis in 1868. After the scene had been set, the circumstances established, and the crowd described, *Harper's* turned its attention to the special rituals. Before the ceremony Benton's statue was enveloped in a muslin robe "gathered in folds

The unveiling of the statue of Benjamin
Franklin, Philadelphia, 1899, before and
after.

Inaugurating the Benton
Statue, St. Louis. Sketch
by A. M. Student, *Harper's
Weekly*, vol. 12, June 20,
1868.

about its apex" and "tastefully bound with crimson cords." The figure
was completely hidden, only the pedestal being visible. Then the daugh-
ter of the departed statesman, Jesse Benton Frémont—wife of the great
explorer and presidential candidate John Frémont, and a strong-minded
and well-published figure herself—ascended the platform and "pulled
the tense cord, which broke the fastenings, the veil fell and floated away,
the form stood forth in its massive beauty and glory, the cannon off on
the hill poured forth the salute of thirty guns…the multitude echoed
forth shout after shout of exultant joy," and the first statue erected west
of the Mississippi "was seen permanently fixed in all its grandeur."[58]

Unveilings of this sort, in large cities and small towns alike,
occurred repeatedly in the last decades of nineteenth-century
America. The unveiling of statuary constituted a uniquely concentrated set of actions to symbolize a far more gradual and less visible
process of construction. But it also made for a special civic event, a
status it shared with major architectural and engineering achievements. Unveilings were moments for reflection upon many subjects:
community identity, historical events, citizenship, authority, culture,
individual greatness. The monument itself rarely received extended
commentary, but the purpose behind its construction, the intentions

Title page, *An Account of the Grand Canal Celebration at New York, 1825.*

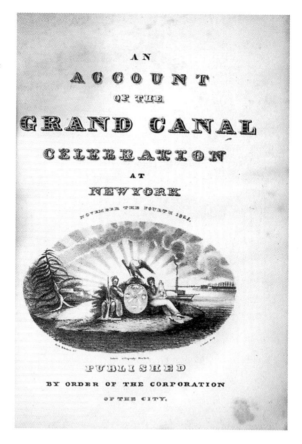

of its builders, these often received frank and not necessarily uncritical attention. It was at the dedication of the Bunker Hill Monument that Daniel Webster gave one of his most important and frequently cited addresses; it was for the dedication of the cemetery at Gettysburg that Lincoln offered what was arguably his greatest speech. These were not literally unveilings, but they were preparations for what would come later. And they were paralleled by thousands of similar occasions in France, Italy, Germany, and Britain, these monuments to national unity and identity displaying symbols that, because of recent history, were more contested than the American counterparts.

A second category of opening raised issues beyond commemoration and memory. Instead, civic ambition was here signified by control over nature and demonstrations of technological sophistication. Bridges, tunnels, railroads, canals, aqueducts, sewers, telephones, and telegraph lines linked people, goods, services, and ideas. In a nation that identified itself so closely with expansion and with practical progress,

Bird's-eye View of the Great New York and Brooklyn Bridge and Grand Display of Fireworks on Opening Night. Lithograph by A. Major, 1883.

Opening of the Brooklyn Bridge.

Stanley M. Arthur,
*The Laying of the First Stone,
Baltimore and Ohio,
July 4, 1828.*

The first stone, Baltimore
and Ohio Rail Road.

these public works achieved rhetorical grandeur that rivaled the boasts
of the monument makers and required their own special moments of
inauguration and installation.

The grandest of such achievements stimulated truly heroic celebrations. Thus the Erie Canal, the Brooklyn Bridge, the Atlantic Cable, the
Croton Reservoir system, the Eads Bridge, and the Hoosac Tunnel occasioned immense civic festivals and elaborate rituals of completion and
dedication.[59] The Erie Canal opening induced a richly dense series of
solemn ceremonies. Its dramatic centerpiece came in a performance of
unification and intermingling, when water from Lake Erie and from
various rivers of the world—the Nile, the Ganges, the Danube, the

Union Pacific Railroad officers at the
completion of the transcontinental railroad,
Promontory, Utah, May 10, 1869.
Photograph (detail) by Andrew J. Russell,
Oakland Museum of California.

Amazon, the Thames, the Rhine—was poured into New York harbor, a
marriage meant to confirm a great destiny and to demonstrate international linkages. These 1825 ceremonies climaxed a monthlong tri-
umphant progress down the canal from Buffalo to the city of New York,
accompanied by banquets, parades, and the firing of cannon all along
its route.[60]

The scale of the Erie Canal festival was unusual but not unique.
Almost sixty years later the completion of the Brooklyn Bridge,
finally connecting the rest of the continent with Long Island, provoked a huge celebration. The event was likened to the passage to
India; its recent centennial, with its fireworks, illuminations, and
special exhibitions, has reminded us just how powerful an event its
inaugural could be.[61] And in hundreds of small towns and cities
throughout the nineteenth century, the arrival of a railroad was
greeted with days of speech making, celebrating, and parading.[62]
The Baltimore and Ohio, one of the most historically self-conscious
of American transport ventures, laid a first stone on July 4, 1828,
with Masonic ceremonies, to inaugurate its line. Immediately thereafter it sponsored an extraordinary parade and festival featuring

Franklin P. Doyle, "Father of the Bridge," severs copper chain, May 27, 1937, Golden Gate Bridge, San Francisco.

Opening motorcade, Golden Gate Bridge.

more than fifty guilds. Eventually the first stone was exhumed, restored, and fenced off as a permanent monument.[63] The completion of the first transcontinental railroad in 1869 was signaled by a *Connection* public and much-photographed sinking of a golden spike and became itself an emblem of national growth and greatness.[64]

Because of their challenge to or exploitation of natural forces—air, earth, water—bridges, tunnels, railroads, canals, dams, and turnpikes often invoked different ritual forms than did building openings or statue unveilings. The ribbon cutting that allowed first entry to a roadway or a

Setting the keystone,
Library of Congress,
southwest clerestory, June
28, 1892.

Consummation
termination
culmination

bridge suggested not only completion, as it did for a building, but also violation of something new and untouched, defining a new kind of movement, leaping across or breaking through a natural chasm. Thus riding on the first boat, train, automobile, or bicycle to pass through the new artery was inherently more dramatic than being the first client of a new store or library. The principle of consummation, termination, culmination, though, is basically the same.

Completion rituals have different meanings, of course, to builders and developers than to the users. And those who actually labor in construction have adopted their own ceremonies. The delivery of the first steel for a skyscraper, for example, can become a significant event, particularly when it is scheduled to coincide with an important date. Thus the backers of the Empire State Building decided to have the first steel work begun on March 17, St. Patrick's Day, to honor the Irish ancestry of the chairman of the group, Alfred E. Smith.[65]

Topping off ceremonial
dinner, Deutsches
Museum, Munich, 1911.

Setting the capstone,
Washington Monument,
1892.

More general and better known than celebrating materials delivery
is the custom of topping out, achieved when the highest point of
structural elevation is reached. This could be applied to almost any
kind of structure, or to parts of a structure like an arch. Thus the keystone had special meaning, placed at the very crown of the arch and
binding the whole together. The keystone's insertion could be marked
by special ceremonies and was occasionally depicted by artists.

In the late nineteenth and early twentieth centuries celebration of

Topping off the Empire State Building.
Photograph by Lewis W. Hine, Avery
Architectural and Fine Arts Library,
Columbia University.

structural completion became still more dramatic when skyscrapers
reached their final altitude. Often a roof-tree or roof-bush raising
would be performed, hundreds of feet in the air. Thus when the
Irving Trust Company in Manhattan was topped out in 1930, a fir tree
was placed on its topmost column. For certain buildings, particularly
speculative office buildings, the roof tree offers an opportunity for
promotion and salesmanship akin to groundbreaking or cornerstone
laying. Analyzing the custom in *Pencil Points* some sixty years ago,
William Collins linked it to the animism of the Druids and other
"children of the forest," who believed that trees contained souls and
deserved worship. This faith later evolved into adoration of the forest
god, who could be propitiated by the addition of branches and trees to
new buildings. In Germany, Sweden, Norway, and other northern
countries, a series of ceremonies involving carpenters, master
builders, and decorated tree branches were linked to roof raisings.
Whatever modern explanations were offered, Collins insisted, the origins could be found in ancient superstitions.[66]

In some cases today, after the press has been alerted a special steel
column is delivered and separately hoisted up to the top of the building. With photographers and newspaper reporters at the ready, cham-
pagne toasts are drunk, pictures taken, and short speeches made by
owners, builders, and developers. When the final steel column made

Charles Dudley Arnold, *Dedication and
Opening Ceremonies,* World's Columbian
Exposition, Chicago, 1892. The Art
Institute of Chicago.

it to the site, joked one observer about the photo opportunity session,
it was the only time workers saw a clean truck and a clean driver.[67]
Sometimes the column has an American flag attached to it.[68] Work
continues after topping out; there is usually more steel to be hauled
up to complete the structure, and indeed, there is some confusion
about when precisely topping out has taken place. "Can it be said to
occur when the men begin erecting the highest floor? Or only when
they finish the floor?" asks one building historian.[69] It is often up to
the caprice of the developers, but even with specific disagreements it
is clear some kind of milestone has been reached, something like the
perpetually punned-upon high school commencement. With all the
ambiguity of a diploma, the being that is the building has reached its
final height; now the inner systems and the outer clothing must be
inserted and applied.

The actual opening of a building might be relatively modest compared with the ceremonies deployed to open a group of buildings,
in particular the international expositions that were hosted so exu-
berantly by the United States and many western nations in the
course of the late nineteenth and early twentieth centuries. Like

Charles Dudley Arnold, *Dedication and
Opening Ceremonies,* World's Columbian
Exposition, Chicago, 1892. The Art
Institute of Chicago.

other building projects, such institutions had their groundbreakings and their dedication ceremonies some time in advance, but the
scale of expositions was so much larger, and their promise of spectacle so much more generous, that these occurrences were turned
into dramatic events of the first order. Chicago's huge Columbian
Exposition serves as an apt example. When it was dedicated in
October 1892, six months before the actual opening, a crowd of
125,000 people gathered within the confines of the Manufacturer's
Palace, "the largest assemblage that was ever brought together
under one roof," boasted the official spokesman for the exposition.
Seventy thousand were served lunch; a chorus of 5,000 provided
music. Prayers, poems, orations, and songs went on for hours.
Banquets, receptions, and parades followed downtown, attended by
dozens of governors, church prelates, diplomats, and any other
notables caught within a five-hundred-mile radius.[70]

But this was relatively minor compared to the actual opening on May
1, 1893. Here the special effects permitted by the newly installed electri-

cal systems dazzled the assembled masses. Shortly after noon, when President Grover Cleveland touched a gold and ivory electrical button, he set in motion hundreds of engines on the exhibition grounds, loosened one hundred steam whistles, caused guns and cannon to belch out fire and smoke, unfurled more than eight hundred flags and banners from the roofs and towers of exposition buildings, began the chiming of bells, spurted water from fountains, unveiled Daniel Chester French's great Statue of the Republic, and set free two hundred snow-white doves. Or, to quote a more rhapsodical description, "at one and the same instant the audience burst into a thundering shout, the orchestra pealed forth the strains of the Hallelujah Chorus, the wheels of the giant Ellis engine in Machinery Hall commenced to revolve, the electric fountains in the lagoon threw their torrents toward the sky, a flood of water gushed from the MacMonnies Fountain . . . the thunder of artillery came from the vessels in the lake, the chimes in Manufactures Hall and on the German Building rang out a merry peal, and overhead, the flags at the top of the poles in front of the platform fell apart and revealed two gilded models of the ships in which Columbus first sailed to American shores."[71] In some ways the exposition itself might have been anticlimactic after all this, but fortunately the White City in Jackson Park delivered on its high expectations.

President Cleveland touched the electrical button in the actual presence of the structures being opened, but within twenty years it was possible to inaugurate buildings by remote control. The spectacular debut of Cass Gilbert's Woolworth Building, so lovingly publicized and imposingly decorated it had become a national event, was stage-managed to a great extent. Its planning and construction progress had been covered on an almost monthly basis by newspapers and national magazines, and its 1913 dedication was highlighted by President Wilson's pressing a button, while still in Washington, to illuminate the building. During the next quarter-century American presidents dignified many such occasions while remaining at their desks, relying upon the power of long-distance electricity. The Empire State Building, for example, which hosted a daylong party for its opening, May 1, 1931, covered both by radio and by newsreel cameras, had President Hoover push a switch in the White House that turned on the lights in the main lobby.[72] Just a few years later Franklin Delano Roosevelt punched a telegraph key to signal the opening of the Golden Gate Bridge, three thousand miles away.[73]

Today's new buildings are often attended with ceremonial gestures whose ritual presence has not altered fundamentally for two hundred years. Groundbreaking, cornerstone laying, topping, and dedication-

opening still mean something to builders, owners, and users, though
they are now more rarely the subject of civic celebrations. Architecture,
in fact, is one area of life where an arcane ceremonialism has survived
to an extraordinary degree. Indeed, the building art may be called its
most welcoming asylum. Scale, cost, and presence argue for a set of
structuring rituals, in order to focus and concentrate collective attention. And where public works are involved, they signal part of the
larger drama of technological intervention, whose rhetoric of progress
through mastery is nurtured by celebration of engineering triumphs.
That such structures—the tunnels, bridges, railroads—are often
achieved at the cost of many lives, makes their opening ceremonies
still more necessary as gestures of tribute and affirmation.

One exception to this enthusiasm for building ritual may seem to
be domestic architecture. It has received limited attention here,
largely because most people in contemporary America don't build
their own homes. More typically, residents and new owners move in
only after these structures have been lived in by generations of predecessors; many of them are renters, and people have multiple places of
residence in the course of a lifetime.

But the move into a residence, previously owned and rented or not, is
attended by various popular rituals, among them the housewarming.
Throughout history house completion and house possession have
attracted special signs and symbols. The threshold and the hearth have
been attended by their own divinities; the doorpost as a boundary mark
or a display center forms a subject all its own.[74] One of the most ancient
of all rituals derives from the injunction to Jews in Deuteronomy, "And
thou shalt write them upon the door-posts of thy house and upon thy
gate." Here is the origin of the mezuzah, the covered scroll mounted on
a doorjamb that can be seen each time the home is entered or left.[75]
Some of the various commentaries on this custom argue that the scroll
was intended to remind occupants of God's watchfulness and guardian-
ship and of their special relationship to his word. Its location was
significant. Such a sign, for example, was unnecessary for the synagogue, the House of God, because those who entered and left it required
no additional reminder of their faith. Consecration of private dwellings
is, then, traceable at least as far back as the time of Moses.

Entry into or departure from the house at solemn occasions—weddings and funerals—is also attended by special ceremonies in many
cultures. These focus on reaffirming the sanctity or the purity of the
household. Sometimes it is merely the washing of hands before cross-
ing the threshold, or the eating of bread and salt, or the practice of
offering new householders symbols of health and prosperity. The

Great Parlour, Wightwick
Manor, Staffordshire;
Morris & Co. interior,
1890s.

"Musica Donum Dei,"
music room, house of an art
connoisseur; M. H. Baillie
Scott submission in 1901
Darmstadt competition.

doffing of shoes in Japan is another device that honors the domestic
space. All these are practical efforts to zone the home, to emphasize its
claims to purity and privacy, to withdrawal, separation, and intimacy.

Within such spaces other tastes and customs underline the home's
status as a nursery of morals and a teacher of values. At the turn of the
twentieth century the arts and crafts movement, in Europe and America,
seemed to endorse the pedagogic value of interior design, moving well
beyond the practice of hanging framed samplers. Mottoes, quotations,
and titles might be inscribed or painted on furniture or on living room
and dining room walls. Often clad in specially evocative letter forms,
they frequently reinforced an atmosphere of respect for antiquity, for
authority, for tradition and the family. Sometimes mottoes were even
employed in work settings, such as factories and offices—for example,
the extraordinary and innovative building that Frank Lloyd Wright

"Intelligence Enthusiasm Control": motto in Larkin Building, Buffalo; Frank Lloyd Wright, 1905.

designed for the Larkin Company in Buffalo. Here, in carved and painted form, in sculptural reliefs as well as words, were expressed "the virtues of work and the global aspirations of the Larkin Company."[76]

All these may be termed symbols of demarcation and presence rather than of inauguration and installation. They could apply to old structures as well as to new ones, and they were meant to influence and refer to broad patterns of social behavior. But in all their variety they are also reminders of the significant role played by marking as a means of taking and then indicating possession. The millions of plaques, tablets, carved emblems that adorn our buildings supply a huge reservoir of evidence. Their historical summaries, sculpted scenes, invocation of heroes, expressions of purpose are modern versions, albeit serving different functions, of the steles which once stood in the agoras of Greek cities, whose inscriptions, as Joseph Rykwert concluded, reminded each inhabitant of "the decrees and oaths which bound his city to its colonies, or, if it was itself a colony, to the mother town, and described

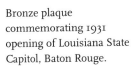

Bronze plaque
commemorating 1931
opening of Louisiana State
Capitol, Baton Rouge.

in detail the part which they undertook to play in each other's political
and economic life."[77] The plaques commemorated the associations and
purposes that the building's cornerstone laying and dedication offered
as performance. But unlike the monuments of earlier ages, they rarely
became in themselves part of any ongoing ritual.

Another such indication could be found in the naming of structures.
For if the birth, baptism, and rites of adulthood have any bearing as
analogies, surely the giving of a name to a building must be acknowledged as a humanizing gesture. The christening baptism of a ship, after
all, is fundamentally the bestowal of its name. And, after certain "raisings" of buildings in preindustrial America, there was a general call for
a name to be given the frame, a temporary one to be sure, frequently far
more elegant and pretentious than any the building itself might bear.

Moreover, buildings are frequently named for their immediate predecessors, the way children are named for their parents or other relatives.
In many cities office buildings bear the titles that previous structures on
the same site once bore, or memorialize the owners of houses and

Naming of the *Wilmington*,
Harper's Weekly, vol. 39,
November 2, 1895.

homesteads which once stood there. New York's Everett Building, or
200 Park South, memorializes the Everett House, one of the city's
major hotels, erected fifty years earlier. In Cleveland, a series of
Williamson Buildings were opened on the Public Square, on the site of
the Williamson family homestead.

But the parallels between personal and building names are not all
reinforcing. So far as private dwellings are concerned, customs vary
considerably. In England, at least, country and suburban houses usually
bear names, perhaps an inheritance of the practice of naming castles
and manor houses, a usage that dates back to the Middle Ages. And in
some countries on the Continent the habit is even more widespread.[78]

Americans, except for the owners of great houses and some whim-
sical country places of the past two centuries, have not generally
adopted this habit. On the whole names have been reserved for collective and corporate structures (office buildings and apartments) or
donor opportunities (university buildings, for example, hospitals,
libraries, museum wings).[79] Some have argued that such names are
often meant to compensate for the anonymity of an address, person-
alizing an otherwise impersonal collectivity. And the naming of a
building, sometimes undertaken long after it has been open, is not
usually attended with the same significance as the naming of a per-
son or of a ship, in part because most buildings also have addresses.
Addresses, of course, can sometimes be vanity operations in them-

Sylvia Apartment House, 59
West 76th Street, New York.

selves, as self-consciously achieved as the names. Hence the apartment building on Chicago's Michigan Avenue known as One
Magnificent Mile. Faced with the problem of rushing aid to buildings
in emergencies, municipal authorities have recently been insisting
upon standard and recognizable addresses for all structures.[80]

With occasional exceptions, then, an address provides an alternate
and usually permanent identity, while building names can be obscure in
origin, misleading, and changeable.[81] This has made some original owners unhappy. John D. Rockefeller actually repurchased a building in
Cleveland upon discovering that the new owners intended to abandon
the Rockefeller name.[82] And whatever transformations of ownership, it
is hard to give up thinking about the Chrysler or RCA or *New York Times*
buildings in any but their baptismal labels. But admittedly their rituals of
dedication and opening were really about things other than their titles.

The multiple-dwelling house is another type, along with the office
building, exempt from the general American indifference to building
names. The rule is, *Harper's Weekly* reported in an 1894 survey of
apartment buildings, "the poorer the house, the finer the name."[83] The
author of this article found streets lined with tenements called variously the Pembroke, the Warwick, the Bayard, and the Sidney. This fit
easily within a broader aping of English customs that attracted the
attention of contemporary satirists and cartoonists, aroused by
Anglophile pretensions. Such pretensions were expressed by every-

Cairo Hotel and Apartment
House, Washington, D.C.

naming

thing from dress fashions to the millionaires' delight in marrying off
their daughters to English peers, but in building terms it involved the
popularity of certain names, particularly for country villas, and the
practice of calling hotels and apartments the "something" Arms. This
convention invoked the custom of British inns in sporting the coats of
arms of local nobles as a sign of their own pretensions. American
owners and builders were subject to no local limitations, of course.
They could wander at will through the United Kingdom and across
Western Europe and beyond for inspiration. But by 1912 concerned
Detroiters complained that they had almost run out of suitable names
for apartment buildings, so fastidious had the taste become.[84]

In the case of office buildings, the name can testify to the size,
wealth, and prestige of a major corporation. Speculative structures
frequently entice major tenants by the promise of naming the new
building after them. As a major space user, the renting corporation
reaps the additional publicity. But these names are simply indexes to
corporate power.

Students of naming and its history have analyzed changing patterns
for apartment-house complexes, hotels, streets and boulevards, and,
more recently, real-estate subdivisions.[85] And they have linked the rise

and fall of favored motifs—animal, vegetable, and mineral—to marketing programs and changing social inclinations.[86] What appears to
be the play of entirely arbitrary materials and allusions can reveal more
deeply based cultural patterns, as well as subtly changing preferences
for certain natural landscape features and national cultures.

With names and naming we have arrived at issues of inscription.
Builders of apartments, hotels, suburban tracts, and speculative office
buildings remain eager participants in the process of historicizing
space and dignifying buildings through the associational references
that names can provide. Sometimes the generic term itself—hotel,
lodge, motel, inn, cottages, resort—comes into question, aside from
the specific title.[87] But naming is itself merely a first step. In the nineteenth and twentieth centuries printed descriptions and graphic renditions multiplied as devices meant to affirm structural personality and
identity. They proved especially popular at opening celebrations and at
a few other special moments in the structural life cycle. Thus the idea
of the anniversary, the marking of historical time, which I shall explore
in the next essay. It is this ceremony that forms the bridge between
building birth and infancy and its coming of age. Since the ability to
read helps mark, for many, the achievement of personal self-consciousness, it is probably relevant that the next essay relies so extensively on published descriptions, maps, and literary representation.

The complex ceremonial systems that have evolved to mark the
commencement, completion, and human initiation of built structures
can be broken down into any number of categories. They are often
meant to distinguish, among other things, the secular from the sacred,
the public from the private, the local from the national. Such rituals
deserve far more careful exegesis than can be offered here. For they
offer revelations about the cultural makeup of the community and the
social status of the constructive arts. As with any rites of passage, variety and deviation are at war with convention. Despite their diversity,
these acts centered around the beginnings of building life. Most of the
building's career lay ahead. In the following essay we shall see the subject through its next stages, moving from the promise of youth
through the achievements of maturity. For many buildings, as for
many people, genealogy proves a less reliable guide to future fortunes
than the nurture afforded (or denied) by the larger environment.
Health, safety, and reputation depend heavily on this encounter.

New York Times one-hundredth birthday
cake, 1950.

2

Signs of Life

IN OCTOBER 1992 Washington's Willard Hotel was the site of a three-day conference attended by several hundred historians, political scientists, journalists, politicians, bureaucrats, and private citizens. They gave papers, offered comments, attended symposia, and gathered at receptions. The occasion was the bicentennial of the nation's executive mansion—a bicentennial measured, that is, from the moment of cornerstone laying. That the original cornerstone could not be located caused a bit of consternation, but it did not disrupt the festivities.[1] Other celebrated buildings from Saint Paul's Cathedral in London to New York's City Hall and the state capitol at Albany have, despite careful searches, never quite yielded up their foundation stones. And in recent years, as anniversary occasions for major structures have multiplied, the quest for the elaborately prepared time capsule, designed to survive for thousands of years, has occasionally been abandoned for fear that the continual digging might actually damage the foundations.[2]

The fact that this birthday party for a building was celebrated, on the other hand, reminds us that its rites of passage do not cease with a formal opening. Human growth and the aging process are accompanied by various celebrations, some of which attempt to mute the intensifying set of physical challenges that aging brings with it. The same thing is true for buildings. In the previous essay I examined rituals of conception, birth, dedication, and initial completion. In this one I consider some of the customary practices and procedures attached to structural maturity and adulthood.

It must readily be allowed that, unlike earlier life-stage celebrations, many of the most important rituals of adult human beings—marriage, parenting, job getting—are impossible to apply to buildings. But there are nonetheless some useful parallels and analogies,

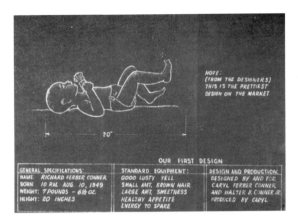

Birth announcement as blueprint.

particularly when dealing with issues of impression management and physical maintenance. These include the various ways in which buildings are represented, framed for visitors and for users, and overseen on a daily basis. Like human beings, modern structures have had an often confrontational interaction with a complex set of technologies. These technologies have helped them become more responsive to changing social and professional needs but at the same time have either aged them prematurely or placed them at severe risk.

A simple parallel can be found in one human activity that has recently been attracting the interest of sociologists, historians, anthropologists, and photographic archivists: creation of the snapshot biography and its more organized incarnation, the scrapbook. Both, in the previideo era, were often initiated as soon as a living human being could be photographed at home or in the hospital. In the United States it was sometimes begun even earlier, as certain birth announcements, occasionally with their in utero X-rays, so testify.[3] Single lifetimes have been estimated to hold within them less than an hour of formal photographic activity—birth, confirmation, graduation, marriage, holidays, family reunions—along with more casual and unpredictable moments. When translated into archival form, these constitute our social memories of one another and much of our self-identity as well. Such moments are supplemented by others, more unusual or unexpected, sometimes even unwanted. Organized within albums, pasted into scrapbooks, placed on desks, on walls, under glass-top tables, inserted into wallets, made into greeting cards, incorporated within invitations, these images telescope the sum of our lives into recognizable patterns, highlighting moments of celebration, achievement, and endurance.[4] The subjects of these photographs—all of us—habituated by years of looking at other photo

Posing for the photographer.

biographies, pose in accustomed ways for the camera. Or sometimes parody such poses for laughs. The recording photographer is a basic part of major family events, and if a professional is not hired, as for weddings, there are invariably amateur enthusiasts prepared to import film and equipment, experienced at spotting those crucial moments in which to identify guests for their ritual appearances.

Building albums, as we shall see, also exist, although in a less formalized and far more transitory and fragile form. In the absence of family members there is no obvious guardian of the building record. Who makes the building's scrapbook? Sometimes a construction record is made by an architect or developer, for the building's prehistory is often better documented than its life after opening. But more problematic, who *keeps* the building's scrapbook? In cultural, educational, and religious institutions, there may well be a documentary archive, for institutional memory helps shape the identity of congregations, universities, libraries, and museums. It is also useful from a legal standpoint, and potentially profitable, for any continuing organization to retain such records. Occasionally a small museum or even a major library puts aside or displays historic items like the silver trowel used to lay its cornerstone, correspondence and funding appeals, or the presentation drawing submitted by its architects. But for private corporations, residences, speculative office buildings, factories, stores, stadiums and arenas, theatres, and a variety of other building types, there is no obvious interest in sustaining such an

Ceremonial trowel used for
Statue of Liberty.

archive. Buildings, in the form of records, belong to different creatures: the architects, the developers, the owners, the tenants, the
municipality, and in some cases, even the visitors. And over time,
most of them change. This unhappy discovery is often made when
buildings are, as it were, put up for adoption or given a new career
choice—large houses becoming cooperative apartments, rental apartments going condominium, warehouses turned into shopping centers. A desperate search for records often ensues, as the new owners
try to discover the original building plans before making their own
changes. The medical history, as it were, has been lost.

At the start of building life, though, there is usually one moment
when youth, promise, and fresh appearance seem available for advanta-
geous presentation, and producing a kind of snapshot album makes
sense. Such a publication can yield publicity, prestige, and above all
profits to builders and developers. During the nineteenth century, as the
costs of distribution and production were lowered and as printing tech-
nique grew more sophisticated, built structures started to inspire their
first baby books, which displayed records of conception, construction,

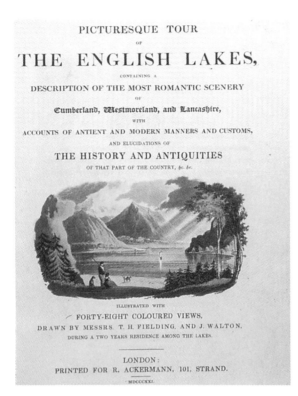

Title page, *A Picturesque Tour of the English Lakes*, 1821.

William Combe, tourists admiring Eaton Hall, *The Second Tour of Dr. Syntax*, 1820.

anticipated appearance, and actual arrival, as captured by many varieties of visual reproduction and rhapsodic commentary. The day of the commemorative text and promotional brochure had arrived, and with them a new era in the search for building personality.

It is hard to find, within this fugitive and largely unstudied literature, the first published album of a specific American building. One of the earliest was an 1830 description of Tremont House, a pioneering American hotel whose construction was subsidized by the Massachusetts legislature.[5] But there were many anticipations, some of them European and quite a few designed for individual customers. Anecdotal histories and view collections had long supplemented established traditions of architectural publishing. The growth of tourism, a taste for watercolors, and a spate of drawing masters helped promote British topographical sketching in the eighteenth century.[6] The enterprising German-born publisher Rudolph Ackermann supplied British audiences of the early nineteenth century with several notable series of hand-colored aquatints. They featured, among others, the Oxford and Cambridge colleges, the public buildings of London as portrayed by Augustus Pugin, and Westminster Abbey. At about the same time W. H. Pyne issued a set of views of the royal residences of Britain.[7] But by the mid-nineteenth century, a new genre had joined these and similar publications, coming of age about the same time as the illustrated architectural journals: the building book, a commercially inspired production intended to acquaint readers, visitors, or potential clients with the history, cost, functions, appearance, and amenities of a specific structure.

One midcentury example, impressive by reason of size and quality of description alike, was published in Philadelphia in 1868. Entitled *The Public Ledger Building,* it contained an elaborately detailed and well-illustrated commentary on the structure that John MacArthur had designed for the ambitious Philadelphia newspaper publisher and philanthropist George W. Childs.[8] The text promised to illuminate the "magnitude, architectural beauty, and completeness" of the establishment; it went on to narrate the project's history, introduce the major actors, analyze the larger design, and treat the construction methods and materials. In the process, the book's anonymous author also pointed out the significance of allegorical and decorative details, admired the building's modern conveniences, paid tribute to its special location, specified the sophisticated machines employed to print the newspaper, and summarized both the opening ceremonies and public reactions to them—invariably favorable, of course.

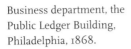

Business department, the
Public Ledger Building,
Philadelphia, 1868.

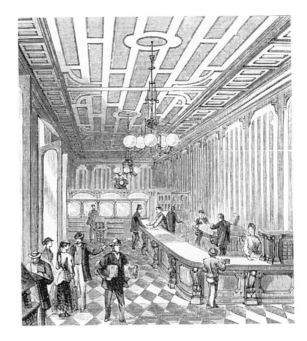

Beyond the obvious implications of vanity and some need to sell
rental space, no other motive for the book is immediately apparent.
Perhaps none is needed. As owner of a printing plant, of course, the
newspaper could produce its own promotional text. And, as with
many other productions of the period, it could claim as the sources of
its inspiration republicanism, American independence, capitalism,
and the values of enlightened democracy. A competitive eye was
always open and could be cast on other cities in this country or the
Old World. "No business apartment anything like it has ever been
constructed in America," crowed the text, "and with the exception of a
few old baronial castles and one or two libraries across the water, but
little of the kind is to be seen in Europe."[9]

Earlier American publications devoted to individual projects had
united narrative history, plans, and presentation drawings: public monuments were a favorite subject. The Washington and Bunker Hill
Monuments had stimulated particularly elaborate productions.[10] But
these texts were usually issued in the interest of stimulating subscrip-
tions or donations and constituted project circulars rather than building
biographies.[11] There were also structural narratives inserted into larger
corporate and congregational histories, descriptive summaries of moves
from one place to another, as signs of growth or prosperity. Again, this
was nothing more than the equivalent of those capsule biographical portraits which could be found in county histories and local anthologies.

Cover, Chicago Mercantile
Exchange Building
brochure, 1928.

Finally, there were notable structures abroad—cathedrals, palaces, temples, baths, castles—that had, by the late eighteenth and early nineteenth centuries, attracted their chroniclers and illustrators. Several, because of their associations or great cost, had inspired elaborate and sometimes fanciful renditions. Among the most popular of these in antebellum America were Washington Irving's *Tales of the Alhambra,* a set of romantic stories set amid the ruins of this extraordinary Moorish monument.

All of these, while anticipatory in certain ways, were quite distinct from the new breed of frankly promotional publications that grew in numbers during the nineteenth century and proliferated in the twentieth.[12] However ephemeral the individual books, the genre was destined to a long and prosperous life. The format could be quite simple. Typical of the more modest early entries was a brochure for J. M. Van Osdel's Ellsworth Building of 1892, later named the Terminals Building, in Chicago. Accompanied by elaborately detailed black-and-white illustrations, it emphasized floor plans, office shapes, and room dimensions to give potential users some sense of the kind of space that could be rented in the new structure. A dozen years later, Pittsburgh's Frick Building provided photographs and floor plans for potential tenants. Building books could be expensively produced and well designed, but these brochures underscored utility and convenience in presenting their structures.

Compared with what followed, this approach would soon seem rather restricted. Newspapers, insurance companies, department stores, railroad stations, theatres, civic auditoriums, apartment houses, office buildings, museums, hotels, libraries—these and other building types were by the teens and twenties routinely issuing hardbound or softbound narratives of their lives before and after construction. They varied enormously according to the printing budgets and the specific purposes—celebrating patrons and contributors, promoting rentals, seeking public approval or tax support, justifying public expenditure—but they included some of the most sophisticated and expensive advertising literature of the day. Mingling photographs, maps, floor plans, and specially drawn illustrations, many became influential as popularizers, acquainting a broad public with modern methods of construction, new building amenities, financing, and real estate practices.

As biographies the literature tended toward the legendary and the hagiographic, heroically summarizing the specific energies that supported construction development and apostrophizing the economic system in general. "The object of this brochure is to give you some information about the greatest building in the world," developers of Ernest Graham's Equitable Building in New York modestly proclaimed.[13] Ancestries—architectural and commercial—could be touched upon, for great buildings were presented as the culmination of long-standing dreams and ambitions. Records set for height, size, use of materials, and speed of construction enjoyed considerable attention. Such brochures became self-conscious testimonials to both the art of construction and the vision and daring of builders and investors. They served to introduce to readers and clients a language that was rhapsodic and frequently flamboyant in its imagery but quantitative and technological in content. Above all they strove to impart to their structures character, disposition, and temperament. "Four-fifty Sutter building has a personality," its brochure, *Art Unto Metal,* insisted, accompanying its poetic text with extensive illustrations of the building's metallic ornamentation, produced by the brochure's sponsor.[14]

In the realm of building books, as in so many other matters, the Woolworth Building of 1913 was exemplary. To complement the dramatic remote-control opening that followed upon the extravagant campaigns of press publicity, Woolworth builders and suppliers issued a variety of promotional pamphlets, in editions large and numerous

Herbert Rudelstein, cover
for *Metal Unto Art,* building
brochure for 450 Sutter
Street building, San
Francisco, c. 1929.

Art metal marque, building
brochure for 450 Sutter
Street.

enough to make them readily available seventy or eighty years later in
secondhand bookshops. They bore titles like *The Master Builders* or *The
Cathedral of Commerce,* the phrase originated by the Reverend S.
Parkes Cadman, who saw the building as "the chosen habitation of
that spirit in man which, through means of change and barter, binds
alien people into unity and peace"; Codman compared the Woolworth
to "a battlement of the paradise of God."[15] Often published to coincide
or prepare for openings, brochures like *The Cathedral of Commerce*
would be reprinted frequently for visitors in years to come, glorying in
color renditions of the mosaic-covered lobby and photographs of the
French Empire quarters enjoyed by Frank Woolworth (who idolized
Napoleon), and offering glimpses into corporate offices and employee
work spaces.[16] These were accompanied by floor plans, diagrams, and
descriptions of the equipment and materials that went into the making
of Cass Gilbert's great plan.

Other great commercial structures of this period—like New York's
Metropolitan Life Tower, the Union Arcade Building in Pittsburgh,

The Woolworth Building,
as depicted in publicity
brochure.

F. W. Woolworth's office in
the Woolworth Building.

Marshall Field's department store in Chicago—inspired similar efforts at graphic publicity.[17] Such brochures served not only to orient people to the new buildings themselves but also to accustom them to reading floor plans and making diagrammatic translations on a scale and with a detail far exceeding the modest house plans that had been a feature of American domestic reformers from the Jacksonian Era on, more than half a century earlier.[18] Edward Tufte, in two recent examinations of the visualization of information, surveys that demonstrate how imaginatively designed color graphs, isometric and relief maps, layering, gridding, and symbolic tables represent an attempt to escape graphic flatland, pays scant attention to the efforts made, over time, by architects and builders to give users and clients some sense of the dimensions and layout of rooms and buildings.[19] By the 1880s the architect, in at least one interpretation, "had become a picture maker whose aim it was 'to make and retain clients' through graphic wizardry."[20] "The time to educate the client is before he builds," wrote one student of the illustrator and delineator Jules Guerin.[21] In late-nineteenth-century America many architects were presenting themselves to the public as artists, masters of pen and ink sketches and drawings. And indeed some architects proved to be superb graphic artists.[22] But as architectural offices grew in size, a corps of expert renderers surfaced whose names are now classic to any interested in the history of American architectural presentation—F. Floyd Yewall, Hughson Hawley, John C. Wenrich, H. Raymond Bishop, Burch Burdette Long.[23] Their watercolors transformed building promotion into an art form by the twenties and thirties. So did other artists, like the prolific Hugh Ferriss.[24] And the extraordinary—in terms of size, printing quality, layout—brochures created for structures like Chicago's Merchandise Mart, Civic Opera House, and Field Building, Detroit's Fisher Building, Cleveland's Terminal Tower, or New York's Empire State, Chanin, and Chrysler Buildings, as well as the enormous project of Rockefeller Center, were matched elsewhere by what must be hundreds of examples.[25]

The brochures, despite enormous variety, tended to share certain features. Most emphasized location, deploying imaginatively drawn maps that underscored the privileged status of the building site and its easy connections to roadways, public transit, the central business district, or scenic features.[26] Some took up the cause of local boosterism, aligning themselves with the destinies of individual cities or even individual streets. There were occasionally portraits and short essays on the builders, the architects, or the developers, along with the history of the project and the civic need that it served. Other familiar features included lists of those supplying the building's systems and amenities—its

Fisher Building, Detroit,
building brochure, 1928.

Map, Fisher Building
brochure.

Map from Rockefeller
Center brochure, 1932.

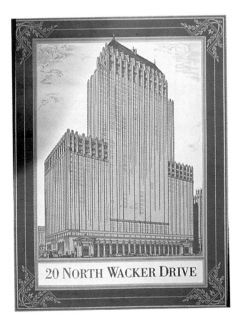

Cover, building brochure
for 20 North Wacker Drive,
Chicago, 1928.

20 NORTH WACKER DRIVE

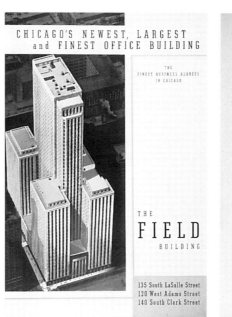

Title page, *The Field Building,* Chicago; building brochure ca. 1930.

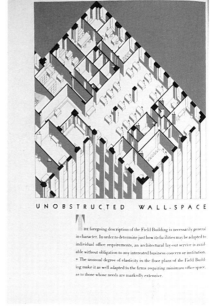

Unobstructed wall space as depicted in Field Building brochure.

Cover, building brochure for Field Building, Chicago.

Chanin Building, New York;
building brochure, 1930.

Attributed to Evelyn George Carey, *View of
the Three Cantilevers: Fife, Inchgarvie, and
Queensferry, Forth Bridge, Scotland, 1887.*

plumbing, lighting, wiring, window frames, elevators, hardware—
along with views of its public areas and comments on its use of
structural materials.[27]

In these carefully crafted enterprises new buildings were given typo-
graphically appropriate expression as well as celebratory description.
The theme of modernity projected by the Chanin Building promoters,
for example, was reinforced by its page layouts and its sans serif type
fonts. Complex relationships among parts, elaborate iconographic pro-

Sir Benjamin Baker, *Living Model of the Forth Bridge.*

grams, and the special advantages of a specific location were translated expertly by graphic artists and experienced copywriters. Some brochures have the feel of presentation albums of the sort commissioned to accompany royal progresses and weddings. They were often produced by distinguished printers like R. R. Donnelley in Chicago or Munder-Thomsen in Baltimore, with embossed covers and on obviously expensive paper; some were numbered and bound as well.[28]

In many instances photographs of actual construction documented the history of the building long before opening. Even without planning books or brochures, promoters of nineteenth-century engineering triumphs like the Eiffel Tower, the Brooklyn Bridge, or the Forth Bridge in Scotland commissioned careful records of their construction.[29] As early as the 1850s dated photographs can be found, produced at regular intervals, recording the progress of museum and exposition buildings.[30] The resulting photographs and diagrams, published widely in contemporary newspapers and magazines, were intended, variously, to promote attendance, to reassure the public about the safety of these projects, to initiate readers into the scientific principles that supported such audacious applications, and to glorify the imagination of the designers.

For the building brochure genre in its early period this kind of

Flatiron Building in
construction, New York,
1901. Collection of The
New-York Historical Society.

Base of Singer Tower
during construction,
August 15, 1907.

technical record was most elaborately celebrated by New York's Singer
Building.[31] Its autobiography featured weekly photos of its progress,
from the digging of the foundation to the rise of its metal structure,
along with diagrams and photographs of its physical equipment. The
boiler rooms, machine shops, engineer's office, and refrigerating plant
got as respectful attention as did its lavish marble lobbies and ornamental isle. Builders of another early New York skyscraper, the Tower
Building, also commissioned an extensive building baby book.

Singer Tower, office of the chief engineer.

Singer Tower, portion of electrical switchboard.

Giovanni Guerra, delineator, *Plan, Elevation, and Perspective of the Castello Used in the Transportation of the Vatican Obelisk*, March 1586.

"Building the Ark," from the *Bedford Hours*, c. 1423.

Charles Dudley Arnold, *Construction,
Manufactures Building,* World's Columbian
Exposition, Chicago, 1892. The Art
Institute of Chicago.

The tradition of representing ambitious engineering efforts—like
the moving of the Vatican obelisk by Domenico Fontana in sixteenth-
century Rome—is an old one.[32] Painters, engravers, and miniaturists
of the Middle Ages delighted in construction efforts; recent monographs have been devoted, for example, to two of the most popular
motifs: Noah's Ark and the Tower of Babel. Illuminated manuscripts
contain carpentry and masonry in abundance, as do many large paintings.[33] These were usually individual moments in time, but in the
modern era issues of construction activity became more complex.
Thus World's Fairs, from London's Great Exhibition on, had been
documenting, both for their official literature and as reports to their
investors, week-by-week progress in preparing their buildings and
grounds for eventual opening. These photographs were strewn
through the histories the exposition authorities issued, usually after
closure of the fairs. And illustrated magazines, like *Leslie's, Harper's
Weekly,* and *Scientific American,* presented building progress in
vignettes. Sometimes an old building, its demolition, and the vision
of the new one were simultaneously portrayed, as in *Harper's* recounting the construction of Chicago's post office.[34] The large number of
illustrated pieces, which included disaster studies as well, recalls the
continuous narrative of medieval paintings.[35]

Cable-wrapping machine, Brooklyn Bridge.
Cover, *Scientific American*, November 9, 1878.

Chicago Post Office. Drawing by
H. Reuterdahl, *Harper's Weekly*, vol. 41,
June 12, 1897.

In the age of photography, workers shared some space with the structure and the building process. Cameramen and some artists captured the dangers and risks facing the steelworkers on bridges and skyscrapers, along with the immense system that was necessary to call these buildings into being. Such awareness was evident even in some of the older brochures. The Williamsburg Bridge, celebrated in a commemorative book written by journalist Edward Hungerford the year of its opening, 1903, had, like most other such projects, a series of accidents in the course of construction. Hungerford added a necrology to his text, listing the names of the dead workers, along with their dates of death.[36]

Nonetheless, in spite of occasional and increasing interest in depicting workers, most nineteenth- and early-twentieth-century photographers concentrated upon the structures themselves.[37] During the interwar years of the twentieth century, particularly during the 1930s, a somewhat more populist orientation surfaced; the evolution of skyscrapers, bridges, and other major projects was still faithfully recorded, but the experience of the construction workers, along with their vantage point, became more appealing as a subject. Thus builders of the Empire State Building and the Golden Gate Bridge commissioned famous photographers like Lewis Hine to record their construction.[38] Occasional workers, like Charles Rivers, who was employed by both the Empire State and Chrysler Buildings,

Charles Rivers, *The Bolter-Up* [self-portrait], Empire State Building, 1930. Amon Carter Museum, Fort Worth, Texas. Gift of the artist, © Charles Rivers.

Up on the tower saddles, Golden Gate Bridge, San Francisco.

Chrysler Building on
Architectural Forum cover,
October 1930.

produced their own notable photographs.[39] A new aesthetic was
clearly coming into being—the men at work theme, defying the
odds, photographed at dizzying heights and against extraordinary
backgrounds. The ambitious picture magazines of these years, like
Life and *Fortune,* were obvious outlets and patrons for such photographs, and they accustomed the public to a series of striking renditions. The building art was valorized both in the interest and using
the rhetoric of science, technology, western development, and personal heroism. The consequences—for national self-image, for the
economic system at large, for admiration of certain levels of scale—
were permanent and extensive.

These magazines succeeded two generations of pictorial architectural
journals in this country—*American Architecture,* the *Architectural Record,*
the *American Architect and Building News,* and *Pencil Points* among them.
Their pictures, along with those of local real-estate periodicals in various
cities, served as birth announcements. Frequently drawings and renderings of promised and proposed buildings appeared, followed by stories

A. Polsicy Company Department Store,
Akron, Ohio, 1931. Rendering by Francis
H. Cruess.

Composite of Turner Construction
Company buildings, 1930.

with photographs and floor plans of significant structures after they
actually opened. Such coverage, of course, except when reprinted and
rebound for large-scale distribution by building owners in the form of
promotional pamphlets and brochures, was largely confined to professionals, though it did provide training for designers and experience in

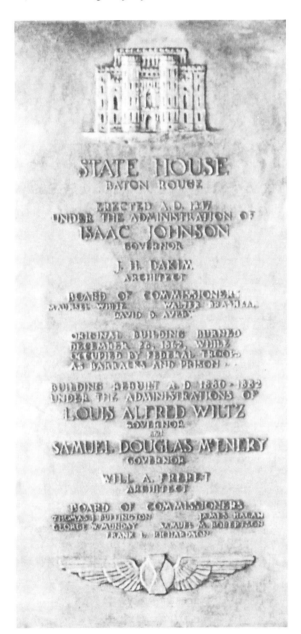

Bronze plaque commemorating old Louisiana State Capitol, Baton Rouge.

evaluating the effectiveness of various methods of visual presentation. And so did production of hundreds of city plan booklets in the first two decades of the twentieth century, many of them products of the City Beautiful enthusiasm that had begun to surge in the 1890s and was encouraged by several of the international expositions. Here the role of clever montage, the creation of dramatic renderings, of well-chosen photographs highlighting current problems, of maps and graphs and transportation grids—all were crucial in developing the public opinion that would support the programs of civic improvement, park making, and boulevard creation that usually characterized such schemes.

Unlike animate species, the living scrapbooks could not focus on family and friends. But there were some options. When put out by developers, builders, and architects, these booklets sometimes featured groups of buildings—the family as a whole—though each would usually be given only one appearance. In a number of brochures, particularly more recent ones, photographs of the developers and builders traced, through individuals, the history of the project from conception, if you will, to realization. And in some buildings, efforts were made to provide internal references to parentage and connections. This could be straightforward and reserved: metal plaques, outside or inside, listing vital statistics and the names of the developers, the builders, the owners, and the architects. In the case of public structures the list was far longer, for there was an apparent insistence that every alderman, commissioner, mayor, and legislator who had anything to do with a project have his or her name immortalized. Because the plaque as well as the building was paid for by public expense, there seemed little reason for economizing on what was often a political statement.

These lists could go on so long that the true authors of the actual structure, the architects, might be lost. Indeed, there were comments in the architectural press about the indifference shown even to naming architects in press stories about buildings and the failure to give them appropriate recognition at ceremonies of completion and inauguration.[40] Birth announcements invariably featured biological parents. Buildings were different.

Some commercial, religious, and cultural structures, though, contained further references to what might be called extended family members, in what were invariably humorous stone and metal caricatures. The tradition was as old as the carving on medieval cathedrals and the painting of murals in civic halls and palaces. The Church of Hagia Sophia was adorned, in the posticonoclastic era, with Justinian presenting it in miniature.[41] Indeed, throughout Europe hundreds of sculpted and painted patrons are seen tendering their churches in extremely revealing models.[42] In America the Woolworth Building, presenting carved versions of both its architect and his client, provided a significant illustration of this device, but there were many others.[43] The self-consciously opulent W. K. Vanderbilt House in New York City, completed in 1882, included on its rooftop a statue representing the architect, Richard Morris Hunt, dressed as a stonemason.[44] Buffalo's City Hall, completed fifty years later, displayed its architect's portrait in a lobby

Sculptured elevator doors,
City-County Building,
Pittsburgh, 1915–1916.

Workshop of Hans von
Kulmbach, St. Sebaldus,
c. 1520.

Architect Cass Gilbert,
depicted on Woolworth
Building corbel by Thomas
Johnson.

Memorial Hall,
Philadelphia, as inkwell.

Building models, from
the Collection of Robert
Bruegmann.

lunette by noted muralist William de Leftwich Dodge.[45] Dozens of other sculpted or painted portraits were inserted into public and institutional structures.[46] Similar customs continue even today, sometimes, as earlier, in a humorous and self-mocking mode.[47] Libraries, museums, schools, and other structures that incise the names of immortals across their facades have occasionally been discovered to be exhibiting elaborate acrostics, projecting a message of one kind or another, or merely encoding the names of some of those involved in the building. The Boston Public Library stood accused by some contemporaries of employing this scheme with its immense cast of learned and literary characters, whose initials supposedly spelled out the names of its architect creators, McKim, Mead, and White.

As with individuals, building appearance and reputation are often mediated by the attention of others. Not all appearances are officially sanctioned. The growing souvenir industry of late-nineteenth-century America, producing banks, toys, calendars, dolls, ashtrays, saltcellars, knickknacks, jewelry, combs, mugs, and almost anything else that could bear a message or an image on its surface, was soon at work depicting buildings or furnishing building models, sometimes as banks or containers, more often just as trophies.[48] Monuments like the Statue of Liberty particularly inspired the souvenir makers, as it did pastry chefs,

Flatiron Building by night,
postcard.

Photographing the Flatiron Building,
1903–1904. Photograph by Robert L.
Backlow. Collection of The New-York
Historical Society

jewelers, and poster makers. The Eiffel Tower, at about the same time,
was reproduced in copper, zinc, chocolate, bronze, wood, nickel, cardboard, sugar, vermeil, marble, gold, and silver.[49] Private and less celebrated structures had to produce their own keepsakes.[50]

Celebrated office buildings, like the Flatiron or the Woolworth,
stimulated postcard makers even more than souvenir producers.[51]
Beginning in the 1890s at the Columbian Exposition and fully
unfolding in the first decade of the twentieth century, architectural
design and the building arts found what was probably their most popular medium of expression, as dozens of pocket-size versions of individual structures found their way into general circulation.[52] The tens
of thousands of building postcards that appeared before 1914, and the

Heart of Cleveland by airplane, postcard.

hundreds of thousands thereafter, not only served to make the buildings' features familiar to many but also added to the scrapbook motif
by presenting the buildings as others saw them and at various times
of their lives: in sunlight, in rain, in winter and in summer, with
awnings on and with awnings off, with horses and carriages, with
streetcars, with automobiles, by day and by night, with new additions,
with new lighting, decorated for special events and occasions, from
ground level, from the air, from close up and from far away, and
sometimes, because of the imagination or the ignorance of the postcard makers, in color combinations and materials that were never
actually experienced in real life.[53] Lying by postcard became possible
on both sides of the cardboard. Some ventures combined the puzzle
and the premium, featuring portions of a building which, when put
together, added up to the actual structure. Again, the Woolworth
Building was featured by this kind of product. Deconstruction and
reconstruction by card, or rendering the buildings in comical scenes,
helped personalize certain structures that, commercial or not, were
rapidly emerging as symbols of their home cities. A life insurance
building in Cincinnati, a newspaper building or corporate headquarters in New York, an office building in Seattle, a hotel in San

Francisco—these became civic icons, more powerfully evocative than political or administrative complexes.

Postcard and souvenir makers, like building owners, sometimes faced the challenge of what to call their buildings. In the previous essay I addressed baptismal analogies and the absence of formal interest in the subject of naming at most dedication ceremonies. In the case of governmental buildings and public works projects, naming might make an important political gesture, though it could come sometime after the dedication. And despite the best efforts of management, popular nicknames or older traditions sometimes persisted. Few, outside of architectural historians, would recognize the Fuller Building as a New York skyscraper; so quickly was it known as the Flatiron that even the owners joined the two. In Chicago what is now the Amoco Building, once the Standard Oil Building, is familiarly called Big Stan, in distinction from Big John, the John Hancock, a few blocks to its north. Sears Tower, recently on the real-estate market, will presumably bear its title for years to come, no matter who owns it or where Sears, Roebuck's corporate headquarters actually sit.

The application of nicknames and the emergence of a private market in souvenirs and postcards—sometimes, but not always, regulated by building ownership—raise questions about controlling the presentation of self, a matter that individuals also must confront. The snapshot is not, after all, the same as the portrait photograph; autobiographies and diaries are not our only sources of information about identity. Buildings had many reviewers beyond professional journals and newspapers; the market often found them wanting on one set of grounds or another. Descriptions could be favorable or unfavorable. The invention of the novel and the proliferation of fiction writing in the nineteenth and twentieth centuries meant that buildings were, in fact, given reputations and qualities that may have been far from those intended by builders. Painters, printmakers, and photographers offered, even when not working for souvenir makers, their own interpretations; despite the power of agrarian ideals, a well-defined school of urban landscapists was at work in America by the end of the nineteenth century, many of them painstakingly recording the massive new structures that were appearing so suddenly in their midst. Other buildings acquired reputations by reason of their cost, or corruption, the length of time they consumed, or the existing structures that had to be razed for them to be born.

The layering complexity of structural images, and the ways they can become a continuous source of critical discussion, were shown in the arresting catalogue *Liberty,* appearing in 1986 to commemorate

Pavement entry, Fuller
(Flatiron) Building, New
York.

the centennial of Bartholdi's statue.[54] Aside from documenting the
extraordinary graphic variety developed around a single image, this
catalogue revealed the sharp contests in which various causes sought
to capture the monument for their agendas, and the ease with which
its fundamental elements could escape the control of those who were
originally responsible for the design and construction.

It is something of a stretch to move from the self-consciousness of
an expressive monument, every inch of which has elements of political and cultural rhetoric attached—Nelson's Column, the Eiffel Tower,
the Brandenburg Gate—to the mundane world of utilitarian structures which serve daily needs. Nonetheless, even factories, office
buildings, libraries, and stores stimulate conflicts over identity and
personality, attempts to shape the way in which they are received and
perceived. Owners, managers, and designers were best able to do this
when the building was new, when they controlled experience through
graphic rendition and ceremony. But once the building was opened,
control became elusive.

Some prerogatives remained, at least theoretically, as extensions of
dominion. Among them was the establishment of anniversaries, to
venerate the completion or the opening of a structure at regular intervals. This chapter began by noting the festivities celebrating the
bicentennial of the White House. It was one in a long series of similar parties, whose purpose quite often was less architectural than
political. Such events might employ a building birthday as a basis for
nurturing patriotism and highlighting national values. This was certainly true for the centennial of the United States Capitol, in 1893,
which stimulated parades, pageants, concerts, and a medal specially
struck for the occasion.[55] More recently, such commemorations, while

not neglecting spectacle or ideology, have also allowed for debate and contemplation. The Statue of Liberty and Brooklyn Bridge celebrations touched off exhibitions, catalogues, public commentary, and scholarly reflection. These structural centennials were expensive to support, but more modest versions occur all the time. Building owners can celebrate such birthdays by commissioning cakes, holding parties, and notifying the press, not so different from recognitions of the milestones of human notables.[56] Indeed, certain buildings, whose demands on attention were functions of their association with heroic figures, have enjoyed attention because of their residents' birthdays. Thus New Place, Shakespeare's home after he retired from the London stage, became famous after the 1769 celebration of the Shakespeare Jubilee in Stratford, which itself came just a few years after the bicentenary of Shakespeare's birth.[57] The jubilee, in its turn, helped propel Stratford to star status on the tourist map.

The problem was that anniversary celebrations could not be held frequently without stretching tolerance or belief. It was difficult to host such occasions more than once every fifty or one hundred years, however much publicists might want to do so. This made the building birthday too exceptional a moment for any sustained control to be demonstrated.

But there were other possibilities. One was exploitation of a practice that stretched back several hundred years but that really developed set routines and a large popular following in the course of the eighteenth and nineteenth centuries: the organized building tour. In one of the rare books devoted to this subject, Adrian Tinniswood has recently charted the rise of one such version, English country house visiting.[58] He traces it back to the sixteenth century and the growth of architectural tourism as a social pursuit, with a characteristically English search for the material possessions of a high social milieu. Multilingual manuals and tipping advice were already in evidence by the end of the sixteenth century, and tourists, including foreign visitors, have left descriptions of being taken around Whitehall, Windsor, Hampton Court, Burghley, Greenwich, and other great structures by household servants and retainers. In the eighteenth century the list of sites expanded to include Houghton, Holkham, Raynham, Chatsworth, Hardwick, Kedleston, Castle Howard, Longleat, Wilton, Blenheim, Saltram, and Stourhead. By 1775 Wilton had almost 2,500 visitors a year. Facing these numbers, various houses began to advertise fixed days and hours of admission. The largest among them, like Stowe or Blenheim, offered specially printed catalogues of their contents and catered to a broader social spectrum than in earlier years.

Cover, Cook's *Excursionist,*
April 5, 1902.

These later visitors were less knowledgeable about the architecture,
the art, the gardens, and the curiosities that were being shown to
them than their more aristocratic predecessors had been, but they
were just as enthusiastic about the opportunity to tour such treasure
houses, and eager for appropriate information.

With the coming of railroads, paid holidays, and regular vacations,
country house touring expanded still further in the course of the
nineteenth century.[59] Saturday half-holidays in several trades, excur-
sion trains, and organized day-trips all were in place by the 1870s. But
in fact, a whole generation earlier, in the 1840s, Hampton Court had

*country
house
tours*

been claiming well over 100,000 visitors annually, Chatsworth 80,000. During the eighteenth century, as writers like Ian Ousby point out, tourism was pervasive enough to influence artists, writers, and manufacturers of souvenirs. The numbers multiplied impressively as the decades passed, and publishers rushed into action with a series of guides and manuals. The term *guidebook* was apparently coined in the early nineteenth century, but it built upon the colloquial interests and travel improvements of earlier generations.

This situation, particularly the pleasure in visiting cultivated rural seats, had no easy counterpart in America, where great country houses were fewer, more modest, more recent, and, save in a few patriotic instances, more private. The great Southern plantation houses were, with rare exceptions, in a pretourist state before the Civil War, and many of them lay in ruins afterward. Buildings that did have tour guides—like the Capitol in Washington, the United States Mint in Philadelphia, or various legislatures, courthouses, and city halls—were intent upon offering visitors instruction in the arts of government and lessons in history. But by the 1870s and 1880s any number of complex institutional structures—hospitals, libraries, hotels, department stores, printing houses, city halls, newspapers, stockyards, certain textile factories—had emerged as tourist attractions of their own. Their management occasionally found guided tours to be a source of publicity and goodwill, particularly when visitors included writers and journalists who proceeded to describe their experiences for an audience of readers. Many of the tours were technical and industrial presentations, designed to show off the ingenious devices that had been developed to solve specific problems or to impress callers through the vastness of the stock or the complexity of the enterprise. Where European buildings could boast of historic associations, distinguished architects, or collections of art, American attractions flaunted industrial scale, the applied science of modern business, the glories of efficient organization, or the magic of assembly-line transformation. The scale and pervasiveness of these tours is established in the accounts offered by foreign travelers to New York, Chicago, Pittsburgh, and other commercial centers, as well as by lengthy descriptions given the early mills at Lowell, Massachusetts, and Manchester, New Hampshire, which had become established tourist centers by the 1840s.

In all these operations architecture was moved to the background, a secondary concern or at best an expressive area that could be treated in a casual and superficial way. The focus was on the activity rather than the setting. The newer commercial and industrial buildings of the late

Cover, visitor's guide to
Sears Roebuck.

From *A Visit to Sears Roebuck and Co.*

nineteenth and early twentieth centuries, however—particularly if they were not, like speculative office buildings, dominated by a single company—were able to emphasize to a greater extent their physical features and design innovations. Because of the variety of services they offered and the size of the audiences they attracted, the enormous entertainment and hospitality complexes built in the 1880s or 1890s—Madison Square Garden and the Hippodrome in New York, the Auditorium in Chicago—were also fascinating from the standpoint of architecture and engineering. Individual corporate settings, like John D. Wanamaker's store in Philadelphia, Marshall Field's, Sears Roebuck, and the meatpackers in Chicago, the Heinz factory in Pittsburgh, Curtis Publications in Philadelphia, all had organized tours in place by the early twentieth century, though once again they emphasized employee amenities, management skills, productive ingenuity, or comprehensive services rather than building design.[60]

As in the English experience, tours began as favored treatment for special groups of interested people known to the owners or managers, a number of whom could be counted upon to write up and publicize their hosts. But the growth of organized and repeated tourist visits, particularly to cities and industrial centers, constituted a different kind of market. We know little as yet about the formal organization of these tours, their length or frequency of occurrence, the training of guides, or, most of all, the character of the narratives being scripted. It is appropriate, though, to note the proliferation of printed guides containing maps, floor plans, statistics, and appropriate information. These were contrived not to acquaint possible tenants or customers with the new facilities but to orient and entertain visitors who might wish to know something about the place they would be visiting just once. By 1910 or so American department stores had become particularly active commissioners of such materials, along with hotels.[61] Intent upon providing customers and guests with services that could be purchased only elsewhere, both kinds of institutions often produced maps and guidebooks to their host cities, along with timetables, address lists, admission hours, and other sorts of data tourists found helpful.

The guidebooks, whose character, variety, and numbers remain somewhat shadowy for these early years, were extremely significant in shaping various tourist assumptions, answering the sorts of questions that visitors tended to ask, and generally defining the terms that would be part of the tourist's vocabulary. Tour leaders, meanwhile, by direction from their supervisors or by personal invention, established the master tropes that fixed corporate or building identity, diffusing stories about the origins, financing, scale, and materials used, dispersing anecdotes, legends, mythic figures, great events, novelties that were part of a structure's history. Their reportage could be as fabulous as the most inventive of travel liars, but it framed popular opinion more powerfully than the reviews of architectural critics in professional journals, while feeding a developing folklore of buildings.

The tour guide gained immeasurable popularity in the United States in the years after World War II. Tourism was well established as an important industry during the interwar years, though this country still lagged behind western Europe in the provision of paid vacations.[62] Historic shrines and history museums—like those at Williamsburg, Dearborn Village, Deerfield, Gettysburg, Monticello, Mount Vernon, and elsewhere—remained in a takeoff stage until the post–World War II period. Skyscrapers and major entertainment complexes—the Empire State and Chrysler Buildings, Radio City (both the New York and Los Angeles versions), Chicago's Merchandise Mart, the Stock

Exchange—offered specially trained guides; so did Williamsburg and Monticello. But the scale of the visitation was still small compared with what would come in the 1950s and 1960s.

The guide services—like their uniformed counterparts, the liveried doormen of hotels, apartment houses, department stores, and some specialty shops—represented an effort to maintain control, in the one case over actual entry, in the other over information and imagery. Buildings also required basic protection against involuntary change and degradation. The realization that there could be crimes against them, as well as against human beings, became widespread in Progressive Era America. Legislative responses were made to control or forbid bill posting and graffiti and to define acts of vandalism. Such trespasses could be treated as unwarranted invasion of property rights, with damages recoverable by law.

But from another perspective, these assaults upon building aspect were more than simply misdemeanors or minor offenses. They represented challenges to identity, as well. The maintenance of a building's appearance can represent, for the larger community, a reassuring sign of orderliness and continuity. Attention to architectural cosmetics, to crumbling paint or terra-cotta, to peeling wood and rusting iron, to cluttered or unkempt or dirty windows, to maintenance of exterior landscaping, all these have been taken as signs of self-respect and community concern. Some municipalities regulate building appearance almost as a matter of public health. Although such ordinances are plentiful among American suburbs, whose owner-residents are fully committed to the maintenance of property values and self-conscious about the appearance of their streets and houses, some larger cities are more lax in framing or enforcing this kind of legislation. Such urban regulations are found more normally in countries economically dependent on heavy tourist visitation, and with traditions of strong central administration.

American cities are proverbially less concerned with and more victimized by the signs of decay and neglect, relying on market forces to bring irresponsible owners and managers to task. There have been spasms of reform activity, moments when public opinion has approved and even demanded that building presentation adhere to higher and more regular standards of grooming. The City Beautiful movement of the late nineteenth and early twentieth centuries, with its abhorrence of placards and billboards and unregulated public advertising, was one such moment, heavily influenced in its taste by the example of European urban policing.[63] Paris, Vienna, Berlin, and other metropolitan areas had apparently figured out how to organize harmonious settings that attracted tourists and somehow screened out commercial distractions from monumental public settings. Art commissions, which in some cities still survive from this era, were given decision-making authority about appearance changes for public buildings at least. And local merchant associations formed additional pressure points in favor of creating dress codes for privately financed projects. Sometimes, indeed, these pressures have moved not simply toward makeup and cosmetics but in the direction of uniform appearance—signage, awnings, colors, window sizes, window shades—suggesting an insistence upon specific aesthetic standards and, even more important, the presence of a controlling hand.

Within the building itself, however, more important decisions about health and welfare were raised almost from the moment of opening. For with all the attention to image, appearance, master narrative, and reputation, the welfare of many structures depended on a staff of informed and specially trained supervisors. The care and tending of large structures was, by the beginning of the twentieth century, an increasingly complex art; in some areas at least, it was turning into a science.

Returning to the biological metaphor with which I began, building health had been a matter of concern for many centuries. And building nurses had appeared, particularly in heavily used structures like churches, assembly halls, and schools. These were men and women assigned to tasks of routine maintenance and cleaning, guardians (the French word for such an attendant is *gardien*) who handled minor repairs, who swept and washed and rearranged furniture. Because many large buildings were in a continual state of construction and reconstruction, the presence of scaffolding was not an uncommon sight, and masons, carpenters, glaziers, and architects were often at work, along with painters, gilders, and carvers, who might receive special commissions by patrons long after a building had opened. Where structures posed obvious risks, or when the boundaries of existing technological knowledge were being left behind, more formal and regularized inspection procedures were sometimes instituted. Bridges and tunnels were always sources of potential trouble, and the history of structural collapses forms a subject all its own. Famous disasters provoked special investigations and reports. There were always specialists who paid particular attention to the purported causes of such events.

What distinguishes the commercial and public buildings of the nineteenth and twentieth centuries in these respects is their need for higher levels of routinized management and for more scrupulous, even aggressive, systems of maintenance. Urban growth, tourist

expansion, the multiplication of large structures with heavy daily
traffic patterns, specialized function, and above all, delicate and vulnerable support systems necessitated the appearance of new occupations and stimulated the development of new industries. In ways that
strikingly parallel the evolution of many professions at about the
same time, medicine among them, the science of building management was rationalized, legitimated, and broadened. And the apparently mundane figure of the janitor can be said to be one of the symbols of the new era.

The word *janitor* had particular currency in the United States, and
its origins reveal the significance of the position. Janus, aside from
being the god of all beginnings and openings, was also the god of the
door, presiding over not only the new year but the entries to buildings. The gates of Roman towns were also under the custody of
Janus.[64] Thus the caretaker of the building, named for the Roman
god, was in essence the controller of entry, determining who and
what came in and went out.

The French institution of the concierge may seem a more persuasive version of this ancient counterpart than the American janitor.[65]
Those who recall experiences with traditional concierges, fierce
guardians of their buildings, may find in them easy analogy with the
monstrous and fabulous creatures whose carved features could be
found on gates during antiquity. But American janitors, normally
with somewhat different responsibilities, remain figures of
significance. It was not, in fact, until the 1870 census that janitors
were listed in the United States census as a separate occupation, out-
numbering church sextons by just a few hundred. Within twenty
years, though, they had increased more than tenfold, and by 1920 the
category of janitors had reached 178,000, 80 percent of whom were
male. Janitors were heavily urban in concentration; in 1900 nearly
half the country's janitors lived in the three states of New York,
Pennsylvania, and Illinois, most of these in New York City,
Philadelphia, and Chicago.[66]

As early as the 1880s levels of janitorial service were mentioned
by pioneer developers of the office block as a significant element in
the attraction of tenants. Janitors testified to prevailing levels of security, for a number of them also served as firemen. And almost at
once they were linked closely with two structures whose character
they continue to influence today: schools and apartment houses.
Urban schools, whose numbers were increasing dramatically in the
last years of the nineteenth century, faced critical needs for cleaning,
heating, and ventilation. Their principal users, the children, could

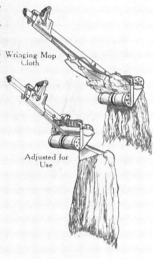
Advertisement from *Building Management,*
January 1913.

not possibly perform these functions themselves and were clearly vulnerable to dangers from disease and fire. "Outside of the principal," wrote the educational authority E. P. Cubberley, "no one has more influence over the physical well-being of the children in the school than has the janitor."[67] In apartment houses, where collective use of the same space meant that traditional responsibilities would not be assumed by individual tenants, janitors undertook tasks that had formerly been performed by family servants and tradesmen. They ordered coal, wood, and sometimes provisions, they saw to the cleaning of halls and lobbies, they often showed potential renters around the building for the owners; they undertook minor but persistent repair jobs, especially for the plumbing and the electrical systems; they received packages, supervised any security arrangements, and ultimately managed the accounts and purchases that were necessary on a daily basis. Janitors, custodians, and engineers were also involved in the increasingly complex safety regulations governing buildings, and, among many other things, in the fire drills and exercises of sudden evacuation that schools, theatres, and other places of public congregation were required to perform.[68]

janitorial benefits + threats

The rise of the janitor to economic power and social influence did not go unnoticed by the contemporary press. Apartment-house janitors attracted special attention. There were complaints of petty tyranny, of corruption, of unhappy encounters with the middle-class patrons of apartment-house services who occasionally felt aggrieved or insulted by these new authorities.[69] Janitors were accused of taking bribes from suppliers of fuel and foodstuffs. Responding to a suggestion at the turn of the century that janitors be licensed, the *New York Times* angrily declared that it would be equivalent to giving them letters of marque for extortion and piracy, permitting janitors to expand the punishments they already exacted from those unhappy tenants who lost their house keys, talked back, or failed to tip generously.[70] What was already unbearable threatened to become absolutely outrageous.

Janitorial controversy was also deeply embedded in the politics of public education. Almost a century ago issues of compensation, perquisites, and control in the performance of custodial duties had emerged as a troublesome problem. School board members throughout the country confronted the challenge of budgeting enough funds to keep their school buildings adequately maintained, while inviting comparison with the amounts paid teachers, or the amounts paid janitors elsewhere. With public funding invariably constrained and contested, the scrutiny given janitorial compensation and specific obligations was close and often critical. Devotees of scientific management practices, students of the American engineer Frederick Winslow Taylor developed elaborate analyses of janitorial work and produced learned treatises itemizing appropriate janitor services, featuring time-and-motion studies and offering suggestions toward standardization. Charles Everand Reeves's Teachers College dissertation included one table entitled "Comparison of the Time Required and the Quality of Results Obtained by the Use of One, With the Use of Two Dusters, and the Dusting of One, with the Simultaneous Dusting of Two Rows of Desks," as well as detailed summaries of alternate methods for cleaning blackboards and erasers. It also offered some broader, concluding evaluations.[71]

But the problem of maintaining large buildings was far more comprehensive than merely the politics of public schools or the discontents of flat dwellers. Indeed, there was one type of building where the janitors were losing rather than gaining influence, growing in numbers but forced to report to higher authority. The thousands of new commercial structures being erected in early-twentieth-century

Cover, *Building Management*, January 1913.

America, some built as specific corporate headquarters but most of them speculative developments, gave birth to a new professional field: building management. Well before World War I local and national organizations were established, publications issued, annual conventions held, and an occupational subculture developed, devoted to mastering the challenge of keeping a building functional and profitable. The Building Managers' Association of Chicago, the first in the country, goes back to 1902; the National Association of Building Managers was organized in 1911.[72] "A building's reputation is to some extent in the hands of its management," wrote Earle Shultz, both a practitioner and a historian of the movement.[73] "No mayor of a small city has greater problems to solve than the operating manager" of a large office building, declared C. T. Coley, operating manager of New York's Equitable Building, in 1915.[74] Coley surprised colleagues and competitors by sharing figures and methods that had previously been considered confidential. An engineer who worked for a prominent building management firm, the Douglas Robinson, Charles S. Brown Company, he encouraged candor and cooperation and presided over the national organization.

Specialists like Coley emphasized the scope of their responsibili-

management as if the building is a star w/ a career

Cover, *Buildings and Building Management,* June 1914.

ties. The Equitable accommodated as many as fifty thousand people on a daily basis—a figure, granted, that was to be doubled within ten years by buildings like New York's Chanin, to say nothing of megaliths like the Chrysler and Empire State.[75] "Its many corridors can be compared to streets which must be cleaned every night. Its gas, water and electric lights, its fire alarm system, its transportation problems, its problems of supplies," Coley went on, "are quite similar to those of a city."[76] The Equitable Building contained, for example, five thousand radiators, any one of which could spring a leak or otherwise malfunction at a moment's notice.

Buildings and Building Management, the standard journal for professional managers, featured articles on the many problems confronting these specialists. Some of them were intended almost exclusively for supervisors of speculative structures—concerned, for example, with renting procedures or with lobbying against ordinances controlling building height. But other subjects, including property and income tax changes, insurance coverage, and smoke abatement, were of interest

Advertisement for Sapolio.

BEFORE AND AFTER

The illustration is an actual photograph, that has not been retouched, of a demonstration made with the F I N N E L L   S C R U B B I N G   M A C H I N E in a Chicago Cafetaria.

Note that the old method of scrubbing leaves a coating of soap and film that hides the natural beauty of the floor and produces an offensive odor. By using the

FINNELL SYSTEM
OF
SCRUBBING

the dirt-catching, germ-breeding soap coating is eliminated, making it non-slippery, non-shiny, and bringing out the natural beauty of the floor, keeping the air in the corridors fresh and pure—*without increasing the cost.*

MAKE US PROVE IT

Without obligation on your part, we will prove by a practical demonstration of our machine, *in your building,* that it will do everything we say.

FINOLA MFG. COMPANY
HANNIBAL   MISSOURI

Advertisement from *Buildings and Building Management,* January 1915.

to anybody involved with the physical maintenance of modern buildings. Articles like "A Few Pointers on Sponges" or directions on how floors should be washed to avoid wear and tear to the paint proved to be popular.

The building managers were absorbed, some of them even obsessed, by the increasingly vital role of elevators in their buildings. Like janitors, elevator operators and starters (or tenders, as they were termed by the census) found expanded employment in the early twentieth century, their numbers more than tripling between 1900 and 1920. And, again like janitors, their work was concentrated in urban areas. New York City contained one-quarter of the country's forty thousand elevator tenders in 1920; Chicago and Philadelphia together accounted for a similar number. Elevator safety was of great concern to building managers, both because accidents brought lawsuits and bad publicity and because slow or inefficient or seemingly risky elevators had a powerfully negative impact on potential tenants.[77] The elevators rather than the halls were the true streets of the new office buildings. Congestion in both spelled delay and economic cost. Their traffic management demanded as much ingenuity as did the supervision of any urban complex. Innovations were continual. Well before

Position indicator board for
eight elevators, Singer
Tower.

1910 came the practice of establishing local and express elevators in
larger buildings; twenty-four-hour service for was provided for tenants who wanted access to their offices on demand.

Until the 1880s or so, tenants in office buildings had been responsible
for their own heat and cleaning; the growing number of janitors could
be difficult and extortionate. But prevailing expectations were completely
changed by the early twentieth century, in part the result of a developing
gender revolution. Growing clerical industries in these years were
increasingly dominated by women: they moved from 40 percent of
stenographers and typists in 1880 to 64 percent in 1890 and 77 percent
in 1900.[78] Both public and office spaces responded, and buildings com-
peted energetically on the basis of the comprehensive services they
offered.[79] Washrooms, central heat, hot water (in Chicago but not New

York), daily cleaning—these were in place by the 1890s in modern speculative office buildings. Thus the business managers could learn from their professional journals how to purchase just the right light bulbs (at the most appropriate wattage) and receive advice on buying the supplies needed for the many water closets, the monitoring and maintenance of independent electrical and water systems, better ways of cleaning windows, and the comparative advantages of competing signage and directory systems.

This last subject is of uncommon interest because it suggests professional awareness of how important it was for people to understand the logic of structures they entered. And it explains the emphasis that was placed, eighty years ago, on effective interior mapping. These large buildings with numerous and varied tenants, along with other complex structures like theatres, arenas, hotels, department stores, railroad stations, many of them propelled to their great scale by nineteenth-century urbanization, were potentially confusing and disorienting. The task of designers and managers was to bring customers, clients, merchandise, and services together quickly, without fuss, and allow easy exit in time of emergency. By the early twentieth century, municipal ordinances had established minimal standards. Anything beyond that was up to architects and developers. Lots of thought was given to the problem of spatial coherence. Next to light, John Beverley Robinson wrote in his 1891 analysis of tall office buildings, simplicity of arrangement was of most importance. From the elevator entry "the door of every office on that floor should be visible; or, at least the corridors leading thereto should be plain and unmistakable."[80] "Plain, straight, coherent," this was the arrangement ideal Robinson promoted.

Intelligible arrangement in itself was not a sufficient solution. Just as necessary was a system of easy information retrieval. Mammoth complexes soon were sporting special information desks and elaborate directories. A series of competing firms designed and manufactured rival office directories; placed strategically in the palatial new lobbies, these directories formed a fundamental part of the information system of the new buildings. Indeed the invention of wall directories, whose entries could be easily modified and brought up to date as tenants moved in and out, was considered a triumph of ingenuity. Installed first in the 1890s and marketed by a Chicago firm, they soon became standard lobby furniture, although there were elaborate alternatives framed in brass and mahogany. Still other businessmen turned to production of building maps or designed helpful numbering systems for rooms and suites. Lengthy arguments about logic and intelligibility preceded a series of apparently simple solutions permitting easy movement within

Advertisement from
*Buildings and Building
Management,* January 1915.

these new worlds. Thus the manager of the Equitable Building pointed out the need for illuminated signs that would point people to the lowest- and highest-numbered offices in various corridors. This convention remains in use today. When certain banks of elevators were designed to stop only on specified floors, shafts had to be cut off and covered so that visitors would not stand endlessly waiting for cars to appear.[81] Indeed, schools were maintained for elevator operators, to transmit certain standards of courtesy, safety, and information control.

The enormous array of products necessary to protect and maintain these structures was represented in the advertisements in professional journals: toilet seats, paper towels, fire extinguishers, sponges, brushes, brooms, mopping trucks, wringers, night watch-

men uniforms, sash cords, cleansing soaps, dusters, varnishes, presses for baling waste paper, locks, keys, faucets, safes, awnings, revolving doors—an almost endless list of products made by aggressively competing companies. W. L. Brackett, a "consulting building specialist, broker and promoter of building enterprises," with offices in Chicago and Minneapolis, advertised in one issue, promising to solve problems of financing, planning, construction, and operation.[82] Ingenious pieces of equipment and special procedures were devised for cleaning the windows of these structures on a regular basis, or for protecting owners and managers from the theft of light bulbs and towels. So numerous did the technically oriented articles become that editors relieved the tedium by running occasional pieces of fiction, like "The Window Washer's Romance," sentimentalizing some aspects of building operations.[83] Novelists and short-story writers had already begun to exploit the implications of daily life within those comprehensive but separate worlds constructed by the commercial office skyscraper.[84]

The superintendents, engineers, and managers, with their staffs of janitors, plumbers, electricians, and repair specialists, were absolutely essential to building health; they could be likened to physicians entrusted with the task of giving regular checkups to their valued patients. Indeed, the comparisons were overt. Protesting the condescending way in which members of his guild were ordinarily treated, Robert Griffith, offering an annual report to the Chicago Master Plumbers' Association in January 1888, contrasted the plumber's rank with the respect achieved by the physician. "What is the difference in these two men? Are they not both men of importance? The one cures sickness, the other prevents sickness. Which is the more important of the two?"[85] Some managers insisted upon daily reports from each department head in order to keep close watch on the building's various systems. Between the 1880s and the 1920s careful supervision was still more important because many office buildings and factories produced their own electricity. Central generating stations, created in the 1880s, served relatively small areas; for decades more than half of the electric horsepower used in machinery was generated by individual plants rather than municipal or commercial stations.[86] The stationary engineers who serviced these steam-powered dynamos were an important part of the commercial and industrial economy, tens of thousands of them in place by 1910. They often supervised and maintained the elevators, compressors, and pneumatic and ice machinery, as well as the dynamos and boilers. In later years, as self-contained, automatic machinery like the air conditioners and the electric elevators became more common, the engineers' task became one more of maintenance than operations, but their role remained central to their buildings' safety and efficiency.

Home owners of the late nineteenth and early twentieth centuries usually could not afford to appoint caretakers; small organizations like church congregations and benevolent societies, and modestly sized retailers, who often paid for only the simplest and most superficial routine cleaning, did not normally generate their own electricity. But

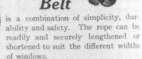

Advertisement from *Buildings and Building Management,* February 1915.

Advertisement from *Buildings and Building Management,* January 1915.

they nonetheless faced difficult decisions in making equipment purchases or choosing among service and repair strategies. It was still
possible in the 1920s and 1930s to buy house plans from mass distrib-
utors, with essential building information described by plans and diagrams. But the days when a middle-class family could confidently and
knowledgeably select all the tools and materials necessary for an ongoing household had now vanished in a wilderness of trade catalogues
and hardware stores.

The development of the hardware store into a cavern of mysteries,
many of them connected in one way or another with house and garden maintenance, was itself an event of some importance for home
management. This evolution accelerated during the late nineteenth
century, though earlier retail outlets, generally for iron tools and cook-
ing utensils, can be dated to the 1820s.[87] Such stores remained outlets for housewares, but during the past century they have become
dominated by the thousands of items that make up the life-support
systems that buildings contain—sockets, locks, wires, faucets, drains,
gutters, hoses, shingles, switches, pipes, and hundreds of pieces with
no easily recognized name—in addition to paints, brushes, cleansers,
screwdrivers, ladders, plasterboard, and all the other tools that must
be marshaled for routine upkeep. The hardware store is essentially a
building pharmacy, both for amateur house physicians and for the
professional general practitioner. During ordinary business days in
many cities one can see janitors and superintendents sorting through
the varied items required for another day's work, as well as baffled
home owners rummaging through tools and materials for specific
tasks. Like the pharmacist, the store owner and his assistants offer
advice about specifics and proverbially exploit a store of wisdom gathered the hard way, through experience.

The janitors, stationary engineers, superintendents, and building
supply companies, the specialist plumbers, plasterers, pipe fitters,
and electricians, the roofers and exterminators can do only so much,
of course. For most of this century America's buildings have been
periodically repaired, cleaned, and spruced up, given new entries, lobbies, and heating systems. Broken plumbing can be repaired, lighting
modernized, furnaces replaced. But even the most skillful plastic
surgery and the most devoted maintenance cannot avoid technological obsolescence or deflect a serious and fundamental deterioration
that demands the attention of expensive specialists and raises the possibility of radical solutions. With personality defined, birthdays
acknowledged, health inspected, and temperament described (if contested) by official and unofficial presentations of self, most buildings,

like most individuals, finally face the inevitable pains of aging, along with their pleasures. The later life stages, for both people and buildings, have recently been attracting closer attention than they once stimulated; they have also been consuming immense resources. Anger, anxiety, and controversy has accompanied these later phases, for architectural mortality—the disappearance, disfigurement, or surgical remodeling of landscapes either widely believed to be permanent or easily taken for granted—is a reminder of biological mortality. And in some cases it is also a threat to collective memory. It is these later building life stages, and the increasingly important role they have come to play in modern culture, that must next be addressed.

"How I deplore this senseless destruction of our historic landmarks!"

Cartoon by James Stevenson. © The New
Yorker Collection, 1966, James Stevenson
from cartoonbank.com. All rights reserved.

3
Saying Good-Bye

IN APPROACHING the last group of life stage rituals it is important to acknowledge that feelings of concern about older buildings, an often uneasy blend of affection and contempt for careworn or unfashionable structures, are not new to this age. For centuries European artists, architects, and tourists have pondered structures bearing the marks not simply of decay but of another age's taste.[1] Many have been admiring, but some were either condescending or contemptuous. Long before technologies entered their period of most dramatic change and made life systems obsolescent within just a few years of installation, older buildings could easily be labeled as barbarous legacies of a repudiated past. When, in addition to looking dated and unfashionable, many modern structures could also be stigmatized as technically primitive, economically inefficient, or inherently undersized, their future became uncertain and survival doubtful.

This chapter must strike a more somber note as we enter the later and in some cases the final life stages for many structures. In a curious but ultimately understandable way, the ceremonial and sensory investment that was once lavished upon the beginnings of building life and flourished so well in an expanding, republican, capitalist America now seems more appropriately applied to the endings. Just as we find ourselves in the unhappy and, to some minds, the paradoxical status of consuming a huge portion of our medical costs in the last weeks and months of life, *interesting* so the final stages of building life appear to be absorbing large amounts of our emotional and intellectual capital. In a world dominated by growth and change, anxiety about and resistance to many tides of change have found a common platform in the architectural preservation movement. For idealistic and mercenary reasons and for aesthetic and ideological ends it has come to be a powerful force in various societies, particularly our own.[2] The forms taken by the urge to preserve are many

Gloria Swanson in the
ruins of the Roxy Theatre,
New York.

C. S. Reinhart, "The March of Modern
Improvements," *Harper's Weekly,* vol. 15,
October 28, 1871.

and various, and they raise ethical problems as well as more narrowly
historical ones. But nothing better reveals the linkages made, sometimes
unconsciously, between building and human life cycles, than the powerful emotions raised by the expiration of a structure's time on earth.

The issue of life expectancy, however vital its consequences, is elusive
in definition. How long should a building live? Does it have, or does the
larger community possess, certain rights to its survival? Do certain building types merit longer lives than others? Should life expectancy be linked
to size, to cost, to originality, to popularity, to artistic significance, to historical associations? We are accustomed to evaluating the progress of civilization by calculating increase in the span of human life. We so contrast third- and first-world societies, and within our own country, regions,
states, and cities. Competition through vital statistics has been a popular
political sport since nineteenth-century politicians and local boosters
struggled variously to attract immigrants, investors, and tourists. But
economic and political competition are not the only motors for such concern. Infant-mortality rates, for example, constitute a source of revelation
that has moral as well as statistical overtones, and reformers have been
quick to cite their sobering revelations in the interests of legislation.

Demolition of Benjamin Latrobe's 1798
Bank of Pennsylvania, 1867. Albumen
print by John Moran.

Buildings, with rare exceptions, cannot be given an infant-mortality
test. Even so, modernity has had very different consequences for their
life expectancy than the continued lengthening that Americans have
come to expect in the course of the twentieth century. Indeed, some
observers must find the abbreviation of building lives as much a tribute to progress as the extension of the human span. Both rest, after
all, upon increased wealth, improved science and engineering, and
higher expectations about sanitation, health, and comfort. In untold
numbers of county and municipal histories, outgrowing public facilities has been a source of pride and not shame. Still more boasting has
followed the expansion of commercial facilities. "It is all well enough
to admire the old marts of the Hanseatic League in Lubeck, Freiberg,
Hamburg," wrote an American journalist in 1890. "They are to-day
the records in stone and brick of a past greatness. They point to deca-
dence, not progress. Spaces given to trade, thought sufficient to our
fathers, are not satisfactory to us their sons."[3]

Admittedly, this is arduous material to quantify. Because of the
enormous variety of building types and the failure to track most vital
statistics so far as they are concerned, it is difficult to offer precise

P. D. Ravino, *The Vienna Ramparts Walk,* 1824. Historisches Museen der Stadt Wien.

Otto Wagner, *Danube Canal Development,* Vienna, bird's-eye view, 1897. Historisches Museen der Stadt Wien.

estimates about building life at any time. It is certainly a challenge to generalize earlier than the nineteenth century. Traditionally most major structures, or at least portions of them, were expected to survive anything but war or natural catastrophes on the scale of London's Great Fire of 1666 and the Lisbon earthquake in the following century, but there were many exceptions, particularly in large cities. Shakespeare's Globe Theatre was, after all, taken down in the seventeenth century to be replaced by a better investment: urban housing.[4]

But even after accidents and disasters, many buildings could be patched and repatched. For domestic dwellings seeking the approval of fashion, there was resurfacing and facade renewal. Before the nineteenth century there were few systems to wear out. Demolition of buildings because they were considered outmoded or undersized was rare, though in certain genres, like theatres, great houses, and wharves, it was far from unprecedented.

Even before increased urbanization, new technology, greater wealth, and demographic shifts threatened older structures ever more intensely, military conquest, religious disputes, and natural disasters constituted obvious physical challenges to the relics of the past. On the European continent the wars associated with the Reformation, in England the dissolution of the monasteries in the 1530s and the subsequent purging of churches and cathedrals, these did enormous damage to the built fabric. And so did the revolutionary movements of the eighteenth and nineteenth centuries and the eras of reaction and restoration that frequently followed. Buildings and monuments became vulnerable to victimization as symbols of systems being repudiated.

But most of all, as a threat to existing structures, there was city planning. The needs and assumptions varied from place to place and time to time, but the inevitable result was the massive destruction of great parts of the built heritage of towns and cities. Each civilization initiated its own version. Several stand out by their scale. In postmedieval Europe, the papal rebuilding of Rome in the sixteenth and seventeenth centuries, in the interests of creating squares and vistas, forced many extraordinary buildings to be taken down.[5] Other great capitals like Vienna converted walls and fortifications to landscaped boulevards lined with splendid structures, thus causing the removal of all kinds of older buildings and grand vistas. Before the post–World War II era, the most vivid, newsworthy, and comprehensive of these modern operations, a continuing source of scholarly debate so far as motive and impact are concerned, was the demolition of large portions of medieval Paris by Baron Haussmann in the middle of the nineteenth century.[6] In the course of redesigning Louis Napoleon's imperial capital, Haussmann destroyed some twenty thousand houses. Vigorous contemporary protests were launched by critics from various ideological positions; their ranks included poets, novelists, antiquarians, and political opponents of Louis Napoleon. Some declared the demolition of entire quarters to be an assault on the history of the city itself in the interests of specific classes, commercial and real-estate developers, entrepreneurs, and political surveillance. The reconstruction of Paris provoked an early popular debate about the losses to social memory incurred by the ambitions of planners and was certainly unprecedented for its breadth of operation and bitterness of reaction. It also stimulated a series of pioneering photographers like Charles Marville and Henri le Secq to provide a permanent record of the damage.[7]

A demolition scene in the Latin Quarter, Paris.

Aside from several older, rapidly growing cities like New York, Boston, and Philadelphia, and excluding some periods of warfare, including the British invasion of Washington and the four years of civil war, American builders did not have to consider the possibility that everything they did might soon be revised and replaced. But in fact, this was what often happened. Fires posed a significant threat to American building survival, both as individual events and as part of widespread conflagrations. Earthquakes, tornadoes, and hurricanes did further damage. A whole series of municipal catastrophes—in New York, Chicago, Boston, Charleston, Galveston, Bangor, Quebec, San Francisco, Seattle, Baltimore, Portland—forced massive if sometimes haphazardly planned urban renovations and destroyed large portions of the oldest quarters in many cities.[8]

But these ends to building life were, if not precisely unnatural, individually incalculable. They did not affect the consideration of when a building had become old or was aging and how its life span could be computed. There is some evidence that certain institutional buildings, particularly those with religious functions, enjoyed a kind of immortality by association; churches were rarely built in the expectation that they would be replaced within a generation or two because

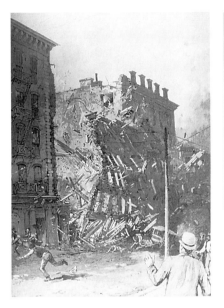

Lynn, Massachusetts, fire,
November 26, 1889.
Drawing by Edmund H.
Garrett, *Harper's Weekly*,
vol. 33, December 7, 1889.

Collapse of the Taylor
Building, Park Place, New
York, *Harper's Weekly*, vol
35, August 22, 1891.

Baltimore fire, 1904.

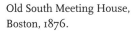

Old South Meeting House,
Boston, 1876.

of new needs. Inevitably enough, many of them were. New England
meeting houses and, later, public buildings, including courthouses,
city halls, and state houses, seemed fated, by the mid-nineteenth century anyway, to sequential replacement; the period of growth following the Civil War made the earlier structures patently inadequate
from the standpoint of space alone. Within many older and richer
states—Pennsylvania, New York, Connecticut, Michigan, Illinois—
new legislative buildings were also seen as expressive necessities that
would testify to the wealth and dignity of their communities.[9]

The older buildings were frequently preserved, however, because of
their historic associations, and so were some of the county courthouses, condescendingly juxtaposed with their larger and more sump-
tuous successors in the thousands of county histories published by
Americans during the late nineteenth and early twentieth centuries.[10]
Indeed, American public buildings have enjoyed surprising perma-
nency; most of our state legislatures continue to meet in structures
that are nearly a century old, if not older. And though they have
endured additions, sometimes disfiguring ones, and the incorporation
of all sorts of new technologies, their semisacred status within the civil
religion of American politics has protected them. In a number of

Old State House, Boston, 1875.

states proposals to take down old statehouses and replace them with more practical successors have attracted strong public opposition. In several cases the older structures have become centerpieces for office-building campuses rather than sacrifices to modern efficiency. Damaged environments have been part of the price paid. City halls, courthouses, and post offices, on the other hand—with major exceptions through the United States—have proven to be less well protected by sentimental sanctity and more vulnerable to programs of destruction. Even here the presence of murals, sculpture, and grand interiors, and a sense of awe at the community sentiments that could have inspired such impressive constructions, have kept a great number of them alive and functioning. After the Boston City Council voted monies to repair rather than replace the Old State House, now used for municipal purposes, Mayor Harrison Gray Otis declared that the structure had an interest for Bostonians "like that which is felt by grown children for an ancient matron by whom they were reared, and whom, visiting after years of absence, they find in her neat, chaste, old-fashioned attire, spruced up to receive them." Such simplicity captured a "spiritual body," which was the essence of independence.[11]

These are only impressionistic observations. The absence of vital statistics in any era—few surveys of building-life expectancy exist, organized according to place or building type or period—makes generalization difficult. There is one arena of practice, though, that has necessitated some kind of calculation about building survival: business accounting and, in the twentieth century, its overwhelming and sometimes overbearing companion, the federal tax code. Fundamental to the planning, purchase, or construction of a whole range of modern buildings has been the concept of economic depreciation.[12] Put one way, depreciation is simply deterioration of wealth in the course of operating a profit-seeking enterprise, the "write down" of the capital cost of these assets. The growing role of depreciation as an economic category reflects an increasing awareness that many classes of property have, as aspects of their physicality, limited periods of use. Not all categories, to be sure. Precious metals and gemstones, for example, have an almost indefinite period of applicability and reuse. But most other objects and materials, from lumps of coal to automobiles to office machines, are used up, worn out, or made obsolescent. Physical wear, natural depletion, and deterioration caused by internal and external factors are seemingly inevitable. After the expiration of their seasons of service these assets must, for the continued prosecution of business, be retired and/or replaced by others.

The English income tax law of 1897 pioneered in acknowledging that obsolescence could be appropriate grounds for claiming deductions. And at present, calculations about profitability when physical units are involved must incorporate some position on the character and the rate of asset depreciation. Far-reaching philosophical assumptions support and distinguish among various concepts of depreciation. Accountants and auditors, along with investors and managers, hold strong positions on methods of translation and calculation, those devices that actually reveal the economic health or weakness of an enterprise and allow for comparisons with others, or with different time periods.

But whatever the specific method of expressing depreciation, and whatever differences of opinion prevail about accounting philosophy, today any building put up by profit-seeking investors, or indeed any building erected for an organization whose balance sheet has consequences, should possess a depreciation schedule. Thus some specialists have divided buildings into varying life classes according to the materials used, allotting wooden structures, for example, ten years, concrete, brick, and steel frame twenty-five years, and corrugated iron siding structures a six-year life. Others have used building function as a basis for calculation. The Internal Revenue Service has adopted its own frequently changing rules about depreciation allowances. Many of these buildings surpass expectations, sometimes by multiples. But the assumption that they are "wasting assets" is both an indication of the pervasiveness of economic categories in modern society and a suggestion that, like biological organisms, buildings do have certain natural life cycles. To a large extent, subsidies, tax breaks, and other official inducements to build represent some kind of political consensus about the potential communal significance of individual structures and have largely replaced the religious and civic imperative as an assignment of value.

Like human beings, the aging or accident-damaged structure has encountered, in the twentieth century, expanded possibilities for renewal, a result of new technologies and materials as well as changing tax laws. Many late-nineteenth-century leases, even for office and speculative buildings, assumed that a commercial structure would last for centuries. But soon very different expectations emerged. By the 1930s investors and builders were popularizing the notion that a building should be taken down and replaced as soon as it was perceived to be economically inefficient. These polarities—absolute permanence or ephemeral transience—were attacked by critics as inappropriate and needlessly restrictive alternatives. This was the position of Graham Aldis, writing on building modernization for the *Architectural Forum* in 1930. Aldis, while acknowledging the need to replace and rebuild, mourned the demolition of several major structures in Chicago, like the fifteen-story Champlain Building, taken down after twenty-one years, or the Trade Building, fourteen stories, demolished after only fifteen years of life. "It began to look as though the life of the typical office building might not much exceed that of battleships," he observed.[13] Aldis endorsed practices that saved existing structures, arguing for their survival not because of sentimental attachment or aesthetic distinction but simply because they could still be made to pay.

Necessary to such rescue efforts was a new group of experts. And they soon appeared. If the superintendents and janitors could be likened to general practitioners, a more specialized set of structural physicians—comparable perhaps to plastic and orthopedic surgeons in human medicine—emerged to battle age, fatigue, and obsolescence. They possessed the capacity to retrofit structures that on one set of grounds or another apparently deserved a heavy reinvestment. Building surgery of this kind grew markedly during the nineteenth century, when gas, central heating, plumbing, and electricity were necessary additions to existing structures. And it acquired new urgency with the development of the elevator. The process of outfitting older buildings, often apartment houses or small office

Cover, Kenneth Kingsley Stowell, *Modernizing Buildings for Profit,* 1935.

complexes, with elevators, became an early minor industry in itself. Adding stories, modernizing heating and lighting systems, moving to enclosed or automatic elevators, transforming or extending ground-level stores, improving lobbies, all these were well-established techniques by the teens and twenties in downtown cities. The popularization of air conditioning in the post–World War II era meant development of a still further device to extend the useful life of older buildings, though the costs of the process frequently were more considerable than the original structural expenses and raised questions about the utility of extending life. Decisions about invasive and elaborate treatment for life extension can, in the case of buildings, usually be made on a strictly economic basis, unlike the human decisions that now consume the attention of physicians and ethicists, but sentimental considerations often do shape the final outcome.

As self-conscious and publicly subsidized protection of aged buildings has become more widespread, it has acquired some of its own ceremonies. The installation of new internal systems, if elaborate and expensive enough, can justify new dedications. Some, like Roy Jensen, former president of the American Public Works Association, have proposed ribbon-cutting ceremonies whenever public buildings undergo any significant repairs. There is a need, Herbert Muschamp insists, "to confer dignity and meaning on the dull and familiar as well as the new and splashy.... Buildings are themselves events" and

Belvedere, Illinois, "Queer Old Building" before modernization.

Belvedere, Illinois, "Dignified Bank Building" after modernization.

"must be perpetually renewed by the rituals of daily use. Without paintbrushes, brooms and laughter, buildings shrivel up and die."[14]

And in fact building modernization, like extensive hospitalization periods, can produce a sense of rebirth and renewed energy. Turning to the private sectors we find that after being closed for reconstruction, stores, theatres, and office buildings often have grand openings, ribbon cuttings, and special programs, although they do not normally produce a new cornerstone.[15] Architectural journals, particularly during the Great Depression, featured before-and-after snapshots of individual remodeling projects, in somewhat the same way that diet promoters, surgical clinics, and hair transplant specialists have marketed their own achievements. Remodeling, of course, is a source of lucrative architectural commissions during periods of economic stagnation.

More recently there has emerged a new anthropomorphic conceit, the sick-building syndrome.[16] For understandable reasons this has

Rainbow Garage, San Francisco.

Rainbow Garage as San Francisco University High School.

absorbed a good deal of journalistic attention in the past ten years and constitutes perhaps the most accessible and popular contemporary application of biological metaphors to buildings.[17] To be sure, the sickness actually strikes not the building but its users. Occupants of structures—often but not exclusively newly completed structures—sealed off from the outside world, collectively develop mysterious symptoms, among them stomach, breathing, and skin problems. Attention, when not turned to psychological factors or external environmental causes, is often directed at the synthetic materials commonly employed, particularly those favored for insulation. Once building-related illness was considered quite rare and exotic, like the Legionnaire's disease associated with Philadelphia's Bellevue-Stratford Hotel; now sick buildings are a staple of concern for management, labor, and government.[18]

Diagnoses are as disputed as they are in complex human diseases, and sometimes no convincing basis for the problem is ever discovered. Although some structures can be repaired, rebuilt, or adapted, in some cases analysts must fall back on chance, fate, or fortune to explain the problem—and here, again, there is a longer tradition.

Notions of buildings' being cursed or lucky can be found in the embedded reputations that structures carry. These, among many other traits, are inscribed within what might be termed a building folklore, described and then mined in recent years by a burgeoning school of contemporary ethnologists.[19] To issues of building health and fortune can be added legends of buildings with fundamental design flaws because the architects forgot to plan for a garbage chute, a stairwell, a plumbing connection, or the weight of books and furniture (in the case of some libraries). Or structures deemed deficient because developers were prejudiced against some kind of modern convenience or utilitarian arrangement, like roof-top elevator housings. Without any necessary basis in fact, these tales acquire validity from their antiquity, their pervasiveness, and occasionally their capacity to explain apparent anomalies. They are sometimes nourished by the personalities of owners and builders, or by a structure's popular reputation. In one specific form such yarns feed a powerful tradition of fiction writing, notably the theme of the haunted house, the belief that some buildings are specially favored by ghosts, ghouls, or spirits. Although the reasons invoked for this often result from historical associations, they can also remain entirely mysterious. If buildings can be physically sick, why can't they be mentally ill as well? The presence of ghosts can, by some stretch of the imagination, be put down to a disordered sense of self, but while many are ready to acknowledge building disease, few are prepared to cross over this next boundary.

But if it is difficult to argue for a damaged building soul, older buildings have indeed been defended as sources of wisdom, voices of experience, statements of mastery whose presence amidst change and innovation supplies continuity with an ever dimmer past. Like sages and tribal elders, they are cherished despite—and sometimes even because of—their infirmities. They function as symbols of community permanence and self-confidence, testifying to a society's regard for itself and its ability to rise above materialistic and utilitarian standards in assigning value. "Old buildings are selling history," one Chicago developer put it recently; "new ones are only selling space." Vintage buildings are "like fine wines that improve with age."[20]

Buildings can also be rescued by conversion from one set of functions to another, and this subject has inspired a whole flock of recent

National Bank of Washington, Tacoma.

National Bank of Washington as Tacoma Art Museum.

picture books.[21] Adaptive reuse, of course, is not a new phenomenon. Until the Industrial Revolution, Sherban Cantacuzino has argued, "the common pattern was for buildings to be adapted to new uses; only since then has it become more usual to demolish and build new."[22] Some reuses were simply the profanation of sacred places: churches turned into mosques six hundred years ago or used as stables by angry reformers centuries later. In this country, as neighborhoods change and city fortunes vary, warehouses become shopping malls, synagogues become churches, schoolhouses condominiums, libraries theatres, banks bowling alleys. The procedures, if dramatic or radical enough, can be likened to sex-change operations and occasionally inspire rituals of their own. Desanctification is sometimes required of holy buildings that change their religious functions. Adaptive reuse can save the shell

Fig. 1.—CARRIAGE FOR MOVING HOUSES. Fig. 2.—HOUSE RAISED BY SCREWS.

"The House on Its Travels,"
American Agriculturalist,
vol. 20, November 1873.

Perry Mansion moved to
opposite side of street, Bay
Ridge, Brooklyn, 1923.

at the cost of the spirit. Although spectacular conversions abound, there
are legitimate grounds for questioning the costs of some actions, which
carry the marks of desperate nostalgia.[23]

There are other remedies as well. As physicians once ordered a
change of scene for exhausted patients—a sea cruise or move to the
Southwest—so buildings themselves are sometimes saved by removal.
The American custom of hitching houses onto wagons and carrying

Ohio State Building being floated from San Francisco's
Panama Pacific Exposition of 1915 to Coyote Point, San
Mateo County, California.

them somewhere else attracted the astonishment of visiting
Europeans in the nineteenth century; in 1838 a Scottish engineer
devoted a chapter in his book of observations to the relocation of a
New York town house.[24] Nineteenth-century Americans "thought of
their buildings as independent of a specific site," Tom Peters writes in
his history of the period's building technology, regarding their wooden
houses "as mobile, industrial objects."[25] In fact, building removal has
now become a science, in Europe as well as America. A whole series of
extraordinary extractions have been documented and pamphlets prepared on their historic and engineering significance. Sometimes, as in
the case of a Nebraska courthouse, moved one July Fourth to a newly
designated county seat that hoped to save the money of constructing a
new one, holidays and souvenirs marked the occasion.[26] World's Fairs,
with their temporary pavilions, served as shopping centers for enthusiasts, who purchased and removed structures of interest, adapting
them to utilitarian purposes or preserving them as monuments.

But there comes a time for many buildings when repair, modernization, moving, or even adaptive reuse are no longer possibilities,

Santa Fe Railroad Station, San Diego,
destroyed for 1915–1916 Exposition.

when investors, builders, or public authorities decide that the structure must come down. The death of particular buildings has, within
the past hundred years or so, been invested with a new and elaborate
set of rituals, reflecting the values of societies that are simultaneously
energetic reshapers of their physical environments and elegiac about
the settings and structures they are efficiently reducing to rubble. The
energy, attention, and awareness put into a building's last days, along
with the effort to preserve its memory, are often far greater than anything received during its period of youth and maturity. Recent generations have taken very seriously the obligation of bearing witness to
architecture in the last moments of life.

The decision to demolish in the interest of municipal improvements
has long provoked widespread anguish and controversy in various
countries. In the middle of the nineteenth century cartoonists were
already lampooning the authorities for permitting the destruction of
cherished landmarks, or merely of familiar sights. The entry into major
cities of railroads, with their bridges, tunnels, and viaducts, along with
marshaling yards and stations, was one major source of disruption;
widened roads, enlarged public buildings, public works, and a general
spirit of improvement and cleaning up was another. The threat to

specific structures aroused anger even in nineteenth-century America, whose monuments were relatively recent. In the 1820s and 1830s anti-quarian John Fanning Watson mounted crusades to salvage and remember historic structures and published a history of Philadelphia in which, one modern student observes, "old buildings become heroes."[27] Students of the preservation movement in this country have described in some detail the campaigns to save shrines like Mount Vernon and Boston's Old North Church. In Europe as well, partly as a result of growing nationalism and lobbying for the promotion of national or ethnic consciousness, early-nineteenth-century crusaders set out to defend castles, churches, abbeys, cathedrals, and other ancient build-ings. In the German states, in France, in England, groups of antiquari-ans organized themselves, partly to protect the dismantling of buildings whose pieces would be reassembled abroad, and partly to defend against native improvers and developers. After German unification, sev-eral cities used municipal authority in the interest of safeguarding an inheritance of picturesque, informal, intimate street patterns and the joys of inefficient but pleasurable movement.

But preservation awareness on the grounds of historic association, great age, and national significance is not the present focus. It relates instead to the larger theme through a certain exaggeration and empha-sis, in the same way that celebrated lives are related to more ordinary ones. Thus the death of consequential and historic structures yields insight into our new, broader funerary rituals and our reliance upon a range of devices and ceremonies to assuage guilt and serve appetite.

What happens when the mortal illness of an important structure is discovered? There are stages, as occur in human terminal disease, stages that include denial, the search for miracle cures, resignation, and then, quite often, a series of life-affirming gestures devised to make sense out of the time that remains. In the case of many build-ings this means, for one thing, exhaustive documentation. Photographers, engineers, note takers, and analysts roam through some of these structures, recording in every way possible their physi-cal details and then, even more carefully, their last hours. The decon-struction can, in the case of bridges or dynamited structures, be extremely dramatic, exciting enough to deserve network news cover-age. Motion picture photography and television allow viewers to be in at the kill. Specialists like Controlled Demolition, Inc., undertake these projects, which are occasionally the centerpiece of larger spec-taculars. In an effort to outshine the Times Square New Year's Eve celebration, Las Vegas featured the demolition of its nine-hundred-room Hacienda Hotel on December 31, 1996.[28] Some years earlier

Demolition of Curtis Hotel, Minneapolis, 1984.
Photograph by Joe Oden.

Las Vegas had undertaken, in the destruction of the Dunes Hotel and
its eighteen-story sign, what was labeled "the most lavishly choreo-
graphed architectural blowup in United States history," designed "to
do for demolition what the Folies-Bergère did for legs."[29] For projects
that are more gradual, the opportunities are less sensational but, in
some cases, no less dangerous.[30]

In some ways, the photographing of doomed buildings can be
likened to the corpse photography that was once enormously popular
in nineteenth-century America and which has been studied by several
historians. In an age more forgiving of sentimentality, and with a particularly high rate of infant mortality, these photographs carried on a
tradition sustained by earlier painters, allowing families to retain
memories of loved ones whose earthly lives had been brief.[31] The
building could not be photographed after death, because by definition
it would be no more. The equivalent, then, was careful portraiture of
the final days.

Although building birth announcements formed an extensive literature, death announcements have, until recently, been far more modest. This differs substantially from human customs. Funeral invitations were once quite elaborate in format, and though they have
grown more subdued, memorial services and elegies are still fre-

quently printed for families and friends. Buildings, after death, do not receive quite the same immediate attention. Certainly there are obituaries, occasional reviews of a building's life history, comments upon its architectural or cultural significance, reminiscences, and anecdotes. In the case of buildings dying very young there are special expressions of regret, although there exists no clear sense about just when announcement of a building's death could be considered premature or untimely, the adjectives so frequently employed in human elegies when the subject has been young. But there certainly have been occasions when the scale and ambition of a structure was contrasted with its relatively short existence.

One of these was the demolition of Stanford White's great extravaganza, Madison Square Garden. In just a few decades it had become a fixture of New York life. The structure opened June 16, 1890, to a crowd of twelve thousand, in the presence of the vice president of the United States, and emerged almost immediately as the unparalleled entertainment center of the metropolis. Newspapers quickly labeled it a permanent civic ornament, a "great municipal possession," a "constant and permanent force to elevate, refine and refresh."[32] Enormous, striking, elaborate, and conspicuous, within just a few years it was hosting some of New York's most memorable events—banquets, circuses, horse shows, costume balls, pageants, extravaganzas, conventions, fairs,

Madison Square Garden,
New York, postcard, early
twentieth century.

flower shows—and attracting, through such diversity, an impressive mixture of classes and masses. It also became the site for extraordinary occurrences, like the shooting death of its architect. Postcards, magazine and newspaper illustrations, and descriptions made its appearance better known than perhaps any other building in the city, rivaling for popular appeal contemporaries like the Statue of Liberty, the Brooklyn Bridge, and the Flatiron Building, all of them still with us.

Yet this great structure lived only thirty-five years, taken down in 1925, killed by its failure to achieve commercial profit and by the expansion needs of the site's purchaser. Certainly this was not, by the standards of conventional architectural history, the most significant young building taken down during this period. Frank Lloyd Wright's Midway Gardens was demolished in 1929, just a teenager, only fifteen.[33] And for sentimental reasons, the much older Academy of Music, also destroyed that decade, the predecessor of the Metropolitan Opera House, might have occasioned still greater remorse. But the Academy, at least, had reached beyond the Biblical allotment of threescore and ten. The old Gothic pile that had served New York University and been home to generations of

2

Midway Gardens, Chicago, designed by
Frank Lloyd Wright, built 1913–1914.

academics and artists (including Samuel F. B. Morse) was taken down
amid widely expressed regrets in 1894, not quite seventy. It had the "air
of one born old," *Harper's Weekly* mourned. But "sentiment unsustained
by money," as the journal put it, was powerless to avert the loss.[34]

On aesthetic and engineering grounds enthusiasts could also
mount a lengthy list of worthy rivals to the destruction of Madison
Square Garden. In Chicago alone there was the Marshall Field
Wholesale Store in 1930, the Tacoma Building two years earlier, the
Home Insurance Building in 1931, the Masonic Temple in 1939, and,
in the years after World War II, a whole string of American notables,
ranging from McKim, Mead, and White's Pennsylvania Station to
Louis Sullivan's Chicago Stock Exchange.[35]

But the razing of Madison Square Garden, because of the building's
associations, its costliness, and its popularity as an icon of the city, produced reflections even in architectural journals about the short lives of
major structures. It stimulated, as well, an orgy of recollection.

Other condemned buildings offered the unexampled possibility of
a postmortem examination, usually to settle claims about priority of

Destruction of Pennsylvania Station, New York, 1964. Photograph by Norman McGrath.

A stone maiden by Adolph A. Weinman from Pennsylvania Station. The statue was relocated to the New Jersey Meadowlands. Edward Hausner-NYT Permissions.

construction methods. The taking down of the forty-five-year-old Home Insurance Building in Chicago, its site taken over by the city's last great pre–World War II office complex, the Field Building, offered the chance to reexamine the older building's claim to be the world's first iron and steel–framed structure.[36] Daily inspections of the dying building were commissioned, made under the supervision of special committees of architects over a period of some months, along with photographs of the structural system. Three separate committees of inquiry tackled the problem. At the time the investigations appeared to substantiate the architect William Le Baron Jenney and the building's supporters in their struggle for primacy with rival claimants, who included Leroy Buffington of Minneapolis. Decades later architectural historians registered strong dissents from the conclusions drawn. The hollow rectangular cast-iron columns supporting the upper seven floors and roof were, they point out, filled with concrete and surrounded with brick as thick as twelve inches. The structure

Chicago's Home Insurance
Building, L. Prang & Co.
Poster, c. 1885–1886.

itself was not continuous; lintels were not bolted to column brackets
or mullions but rested on the bearing surfaces. This was not a rigid,
self-supporting iron skeleton, independent of the masonry; the technical accomplishment, one recent historian has insisted, was primitive compared to the work of Eiffel and Sédille in France.

But the actual historical status enjoyed by the Home Insurance may
be less significant than the investigation itself, an extremely elaborate
effort to exploit the opportunity of its planned destruction by undertak-
ing a pathological examination. And it was not an isolated event. Just
as physicians have seized upon the postmortem as an instrument to
learn more about disease, so engineers, architects, and historians have
taken the increasingly available experience of planned demise in order
to get answers to structural questions. Other close observers have pur-
sued the details of disintegration on aesthetic grounds. The dangers

Dismantlement of the
Chicago Stock Exchange
Building staircase.
Photograph by Richard
Nickel, 1972.

Stencil from Trading Room of demolished
Chicago Stock Exchange, Adler and
Sullivan, partnership 1883–1895. The Art
Institute of Chicago.

Dealer in secondhand building materials, *Harper's Weekly*, vol. 33, October 19, 1889.

that can accompany the exercise were demonstrated twenty years ago by the tragic death of Richard Nickel, the architectural photographer who was shooting the last days of Louis Sullivan's Stock Exchange Building in Chicago and was found dead in its collapsing ruins.[37] The surviving photographs constitute Nickel's memorial and provide, for those born too late to see the building in operation, something of a surrogate. The only thing lacking is a living will.

But in fact, the destiny of the Stock Exchange Building serves as something of an emblem for the life-after-death possibilities condemned buildings now confront. Much like the Hapsburgs, whose hearts were buried in one place while their bodies were interred in another, the Stock Exchange was distributed in pieces after its destruction. The trading floor was reassembled to become part of the permanent exhibition of the Art Institute of Chicago; the entry arch, after some apparent interest expressed by New York institutions, was reerected outside the Art Institute; the elevator grilles, doorknobs, stencils, and other pieces of Louis Sullivan–designed ironwork can be found in homes, offices, and museums in different sections of the country. Parts of historic buildings function today much as religious relics once did, as evidence of the true faith and demonstrations of commitment, to be displayed, honored, occasionally adored, and, perhaps most important of all, hawked for profit.

Just as they did in the era of the Reformation, quarrels break out over the sale and worship of the relics. Entire companies do little more than sell, to architects, interior decorators, landscapers, and interested lay people, salvaged pieces from wrecked buildings. As a business, in the

Hartford Times Building, 1919–1920, Donn
Barber, architect, incorporated columns
from Stanford White's demolished Madison
Square Presbyterian Church.

United States at least, wrecking retrieval is now well over one hundred
years old, though its earlier years were distinguished less by sentiment
than by economic interest. In 1889 Julian Ralph was telling readers of
Harper's Weekly about dealers in secondhand buildings, specialists in a
"higher grade of builders' refuse," who took old buildings apart carefully
and "save[d] the lintels, mantels, doors, window-frames, stairs, and the
rest, clean[ed] the old bricks carefully, and put all the parts on exhibition
in their yards uptown, precisely as other merchants display new wares in
store windows." [38] A lot of money could be made even then. The
Chicago House Wrecking Company was organized in 1892 to dismantle
the World's Columbian Exposition, an eighteen-month job, and became
so successful at removal and sales of material that it went on to pull
down World's Fairs in Omaha, Buffalo, and St. Louis, as well as hotels
and government buildings. The Illinois Theater in Chicago was built
from the recycled wreckage of the United States Post Office building
there. The company boasted in 1906 of performing "an extraordinary
and unique function in the mercantile world," redirecting "to the chan-
nels of industry enormous quantities of highly valuable materials."[39]

The Soane Museum, London.

Contemporaries marveled at the scale of such efforts. "It is almost as much of a job to get rid of a big expo as it is to create one," wrote a Chicago journalist in 1905, "and it is even more fun to watch the wreckers tearing down a building than it is to see the builders put one up. Destruction is more entertaining than creation." But there is also, he added, "a melancholy aspect to the question, a pathetic and a profound sense of regret, to see magnificent buildings torn to pieces."[40]

Such views, however, did not dominate. Wreckers were in business to reuse building parts elsewhere. But by the 1920s, as the value of old copper fittings, pipes, bricks, and porcelain fixtures increased, interest had grown in salvaging parts of historic buildings for their own sake. The facade of New York City's Assay Building was reconstructed for the Metropolitan Museum's American Wing; Stanford White's notable Madison Avenue Presbyterian Church gained new life as the facade for the *Hartford Times* building in Connecticut.[41] Despite the increasing cost of taking down enormous and complex structures, wreckers paid large sums to dismantle buildings, reselling everything from steel beams and plate glass to marble mantels and radiators.[42] Building columns were occasionally used as memorial monuments, while facade granite and marble were recycled into grave markers. Salvage rights remained significant. With today's

Architectural cast gallery, Carnegie
Institute, Pittsburgh.

newly popular interest in authorship, salvage indeed has become an
even bigger business, fragment rescuers advertising their wares in
the pages of antiques magazines and interior decorating journals.

In fact, as the number of major deceased structures increases, so
arrangements for their appropriate interment and memorialization
become more varied. And here one enters a growth industry whose general shape has been recently absorbing many anthropologists and historians: museumification, creation of institutional venues for study, tribute
paying, and social experience. As a recently published essay points out,
the architectural museum has more than a two-hundred-year history by
now, tracing its pedigree, in certain ways, back to collectors of casts and
fragments of the late eighteenth and early nineteenth centuries, to
figures like Alexandre Lenoir, director of the short-lived Musée des
Monuments Français in revolutionary and Napoleonic Paris, to Sir John
Soane, London architect and collector, and to George Wightwick and his
landscape of memories.[43] In the late nineteenth and twentieth centuries
these efforts were followed up by great national museums, indoor and
outdoor, in England, France, and Scandinavia. Many of these, like such
tourist shrines in this country as Plymouth Plantation or Historic
Deerfield, had as their objective the recovery of some historical temper, a
sentimentalized quest for a more appealing time and place. These museums have often sought to preserve a vanishing heritage on ideological,

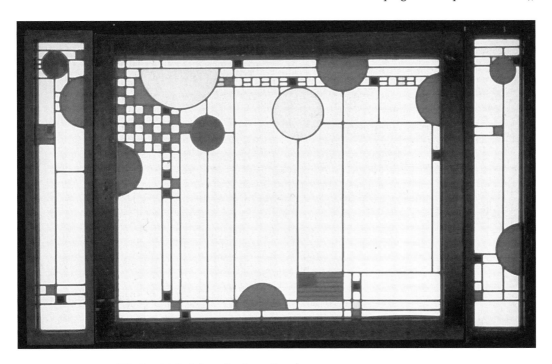

Window triptych from the Avery Coonley
Playhouse, Riverside, Illinois, by Frank
Lloyd Wright, now in the Art Institute of
Chicago.

racial, nationalist, or professional grounds. Such motives also fueled the
feverish installation of period rooms in art and history museums, particularly during the 1920s. It was during that decade also, with creation of
the Cloisters in Manhattan, Dearborn Village near Detroit, and Colonial
Williamsburg in Virginia, that service to this larger sensibility reached an
intensive peak in the United States.[44]

But these efforts were, on the whole, concerned with evocations of
the past. They featured fragments from buildings that, in general, were
already in ruins, buried in debris, about to be sold or taken down, or
surrounded by landscapes that neither nurtured nor noticed them.
While recent attention to building display has sustained such connections, there are also real differences. For one thing, the relationship
between the dismantling of the structure or site and the display of its
remains or reconstruction is often direct and intimate. Indeed, plans for
some forms of ritual preservation are often in place before actual
destruction occurs, much like a prepaid burial arrangement.[45] In other
instances, it is the profit to be made from the sale or gift of architectural
relics that stimulates the dismantling process in the first place. The

Fragments Gallery, Art Institute of Chicago.

story of Frank Lloyd Wright homes divested of their stained-glass windows, which go immediately into private or institutional collections, suggests how tax-subsidized avarice can damage extraordinary structures. "Contrary to the rule of geometry that the whole is equal to the sum of its parts," notes Hugh Howard, "the parts of a Wright house are worth more than the house can be worth."[46] Owners vandalize the living structure to profit by sale of its body parts. Or the body parts disappear more gradually. Frank Lloyd Wright is not the only American designer whose houses suffer this fate. According to the *New York Times,* the first house of the Arts and Crafts master Gustav Stickley, in Syracuse, was sold recently for $138,000 less than the house's original ten-foot sideboard had brought at auction. Another of his houses, in New Jersey, badly needed help to survive. "It is one of the paradoxes of the marketplace," noted a reporter, "that the cost of saving two Craftsman monuments is less than the price of one Craftsman sideboard."[47] One student of medieval relics has pointed out that the remains of the venerated were sought even while they were alive, meaning that "the danger of someone murdering an aging holy man in order to acquire his relics, or at least stealing his remains as soon as he was dead was ever present."[48] The parallel doesn't seem too outlandish.

But whether reinstallation is the cause or the consequence of dismantling, the fact that external and interior designs are deemed worthy of museum presentation within several decades of their completion suggests the highly intimate contemporary relationship between creation and museumification. It also underscores the temporal fragility of even the most celebrated and expensive of commissions.[49] Fragment galleries, such as can be found in the Art Institute of Chicago, feature, in the place of antique casts of statue-laden facades, elevator grilles, terra-cotta ornaments, light fixtures, planters, and radiators, most of them products of nineteenth- and twentieth-century technology.

Other devices for presentation outside museum walls have also gained currency.[50] Foundations, trusts, and specially created agencies can now receive buildings, along with the necessary support endowments, then maintain them in their basic relation to the larger environment and open them to visitation. The Society for the Preservation of New England Antiquities operates a whole stable of these properties, but it faces the problem confronting any memorializer of persons or things: selecting the moment to freeze for perpetual contemplation. Like the commissioners of the Elvis Presley postage stamp, preservation authorities have to choose a life phase to immortalize. Because most settings are layered in time, reflecting the taste of different eras, this is often a difficult problem. It is further complicated by the need to connect with a personal or family life history that frequently makes the preservation site of interest to the visiting public. Short lives make for easy solutions, when only one generation or one group of decisions can be held responsible for the entire design and its coordination.

With all the bitter debates and innovative strategies that have marked the past few decades, Americans are still only beginning to confront the problems of maintaining buildings as monuments. Or to recognize how many of their most cherished landmarks lived by a commercial/industrial ethos that had at its heart promotional expressiveness or productive efficiency rather than religious awe or political reverence. In 1993 newspapers ran stories entitled "So what do you do with an obsolete skyscraper?"—specifically, 40 Wall Street, for some months in 1929 the tallest building in the world.[51] This Craig Severance structure had been engaged in a head-to-head competition with the Chrysler Building for the title while both were under construction. Losing the championship may have been a bad omen. By the 1990s, facing an almost entirely vacant interior, with obsolete equipment and floor plans unpromising for conversion, building owners confronted some harsh options: the building could come down, be rather expensively transformed into housing, or preserved, at least in part, as some kind of monument to architectural hubris. When land values don't justify demolition costs and

Prairie Avenue, Chicago, surviving mansion.

confident investors are not waiting to create another project, public authorities might become responsible for removing a potential danger. One alternative, to leave these huge observation towers dotting older cities, empty vessels marking ambitions of earlier generations, mingling living and dead skyscrapers, raises the question of whether urban centers may not, in future, come to host building cemeteries in their central areas. The photographer and critic Camilo José Vergara proposes just this for Detroit, the "third largest concentration of pre-Depression skyscrapers in the world." Instead of razing the empty office towers "we could transform the nearly one hundred troubled buildings into a grand national historic park of play and wonder, an urban Monument Valley."[52]

In fact, a version of this idea has already appeared. During the past decade or so Chicago has developed a rather unusual architectural memorial park. If it is still unique, it may not be for long. Prairie Avenue once constituted the city's millionaire row; a century ago it contained the elaborately conceived residences of the city's economic elite. A mile or two from the downtown, close to the lake, near handsome boulevards for carriage driving, it was a highly desirable area for Chicagoans in the decades after the Great Fire. It was here that H. H. Richardson erected, in the 1880s, his house for the Glessner family. Within a short distance lived the George Pullmans, the William Kimballs, the Marshall Fields, the Philip Armours, and other barons of finance and industry.

As the surrounding area around changed enormously in the twentieth century, most of the houses were pulled down until just a few remained, juxtaposed with large, weed-infested lots. Respecting the

Prairie Avenue, Chicago.

importance of Glessner House, now a focus of preservation groups and architectural bodies, and seeking to stimulate tourist response, the city of Chicago decided to dress up the avenue with a restored cobblestone surface, gas lighting, and at least one house importation. The oldest surviving house in the city, the Widow Clarke house, had originally stood near the new district but had been moved during the nineteenth century. Now it could return to its old haunts, considerably changed in the interim, of course. There was no money to erect facsimiles of the mansions that had been taken down. But there was still some fencing, so plans were made to put up, where the entry gates would have stood, a series of large photographs of the houses that had once lined the streets, along with short biographies of the families that had built and lived within them. This is, essentially, a memorial park, whose tombstones have photographs on them, in the tradition of many European cemeteries.

Chicago's turn to old houses as evidence for its history was belated. Addressing Chicagoans in the late nineteenth century Wendell Phillips, the noted Boston orator and radical abolitionist, advised residents of "that boastful city" that they insufficiently valued their early homes. Take your first house, "cover it with glass and gild it with fine gold," Phillips urged, and it would more than repay any cost. But the prophet was not heeded, and by the late 1880s the private investors were forced to import treasured relics from elsewhere, paying for bricks to be brought up from the Civil War Libby Prison in Richmond, to be relaid on the shores of Lake Michigan. At the Columbian Exposition of 1893, invitations were issued to the family of Robert Burns to send someone who might take up temporary residence in a replica of the poet's cottage. One aggressive

Old North Church replica,
Forest Lawn Cemetery, Los
Angeles.

Little Church of the
Flowers, Forest Lawn
Cemetery, postcard.

promoter invaded Massachusetts, according to an indignant Yankee, seeking to purchase, in Salem, the birthplace of Hawthorne for reconstruction on the fairgrounds; the locals refused.[53]

There are many more recent analogues. In Japan, Nagoya's Meiji Village, for example, displays portions of buildings, like Frank Lloyd Wright's Imperial Hotel, reconstructed (from dismantled fragments) to show visitors what the original must have felt like. Worldly visitors to such sites might recall Forest Lawn, the California cemetery, and its penchant for constructing replicas (rather than reconstructing originals) of famous landmarks like the Old North Church. This practice is new to neither this country nor this century. It has an ancient origin in proposals to create as monuments portions of famous buildings and in the custom of incorporating, within special landscapes, copies of celebrated buildings.

World's Fairs, as we have seen, were favored spots for such enterprises. Chicago's Columbian Exposition contained a number of them, not merely as tourist attractions but as exhibition halls and state headquarters. For that fair Massachusetts was represented by a replica of the John Hancock house on Beacon Hill, Virginia sported a re-created

Charles Dudley Arnold,
Pennsylvania Building,
World's Columbian
Exposition, Chicago, 1892.
The Art Institute of
Chicago.

Charles Dudley Arnold, *Virginia Building,*
World's Columbian Exposition, Chicago,
1892. The Art Institute of Chicago.

Mount Vernon, and Pennsylvania reconstructed Independence Hall, especially appropriate because the Liberty Bell traveled to Chicago from Philadelphia, to be viewed by the faithful.[54] The Japanese built copies of several ancient landmarks as their presentation on the Wooded Island of the Exposition. Other foreign governments also

Charles Dudley Arnold,
French Government Building,
World's Columbian
Exposition, Chicago, 1892.
The Art Institute of
Chicago.

Charles Dudley Arnold, *Ho-o-den Japanese
Exhibition,* World's Columbian Exposition,
Chicago, 1892. The Art Institute of
Chicago.

commissioned replicas of palaces, castles, and great houses. The
Tennessee Centennial of 1898, held in Nashville, featured a copy, in
wood, of the Parthenon, so popular an attraction that it was redone in
stone and still stands in Centennial Park. College campuses, city
parks, and cemeteries all were sites for elaborate reconstructions,
while in today's internationalized tourist culture it is possible to find
versions of the Taj Mahal, the Eiffel Tower, and the Trianon in various
parts of the world. Las Vegas is particularly rich in its replications,
incorporating the allusions within larger pastiches.

Where full-scale copies prove impractical, links with famous monuments are sustained by talismanic relics. These are not the dismem-

New York, N.Y., under
construction in
Las Vegas.

bering techniques employed for buildings like the Chicago Stock
Exchange, recognizable portions of the design and its ornament
incorporated as accent marks or reconstructed as major memorials,
but true relics that superficially resemble any other piece of similarly
constituted stone. Without their labels or inscriptions for pilgrims to
read, they would be entirely unremarkable. And the viewer must, of
course, like the churchgoer before the relics of a saint, take on faith
the authenticity of the object's true origin.

The quantity of buildings in America that have incorporated within
them pieces of celebrated structures is not known. Quite a few nineteenth-century structures, including the Washington Monument,
adopted the custom. Almost two hundred carved tribute blocks can be
found on its inside walls, including a block of Pentelic marble from
the Parthenon.[55] The city of Chicago contains several twentieth-century
versions. The most notable among them, the *Tribune* building of the
early twenties, features a wall containing pieces of the Great Wall of
China, Cologne Cathedral, Westminster Abbey, Hagia Sophia,
Harvard's Massachusetts Hall, Luther's Wartburg, St. Paul's Cathedral,
and a series of other, mainly religious monuments. The Chicago
Theological Seminary, seven miles south, in a courtyard built about the
same time, incorporates stones from natural as well as man-made
venues, chipped off pieces from King Solomon's quarries, Plymouth
Rock, and the Great Divide incorporated into its cloister alongside fragments from the Wartburg and the cornerstone of an early Christian
chapel near Hebron. The Paramount Building in New York, also constructed during the twenties, featured such souvenirs in its lobby.
More obscure buildings could also be represented, if there were special

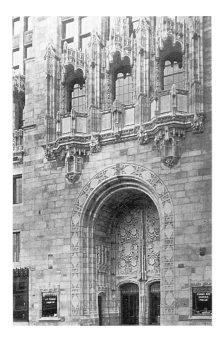

Detail, main entrance,
Chicago Tribune Building.

Fragment of Plymouth
Rock in Chicago
Theological Seminary.

reasons. Thus a new Cleveland Masonic temple in 1886 proudly
placed above the entrance arch to its chapter room the keystone from
the doorway of the first lodge rooms built there, sixty years earlier, discovered by workmen while razing the foundation of a barn.

From one standpoint these fragments might well be considered as
part of the first phase of building life, conferring dignity, authority, and
significance on new structures by associating them with older ones.
The stones are amulets, architectural charm bracelets saluting distant
connections and revered relatives. But from another angle the custom
can be defended as a survivalist strategy for the older monuments,
granting their organ parts new and protected bodies even while their
larger fabrics have been damaged or renovated. Such, at least, has been
the argument of a number of enthusiasts, some of whom have not
been above the practice of hastening the death of a building in order to
display (or to market) its parts.

Building ancestor worship has been both an aesthetic and a nostalgic sensibility for a long time. For centuries it was popular to pro-
claim the view that copies of older monuments were bound to outdo
new versions in a contemporary style. And more recently critics have
pointed to the poverty of imagination and the meanness of spirit that

Cartoon from *Look* magazine, August 11, 1964, p. 83.

have governed new versions of older institutions. For a whole uni-verse of specific cases—the replacements of Pennsylvania Station and the Stanford White Madison Square Garden, for example—there seems little question that suspicions of degeneracy were well founded. But in many others—one might point to the charming but also inefficient and not invariably handsome library buildings adapted, at great expense to present needs, to say nothing of Old Mains on university campuses—the cost of installing the life-support systems has been staggering and has diverted energy and attention from other, perhaps more useful undertakings.

Indeed, recognition that disintegration and dissolution are part of the natural building cycle has, paradoxically, become more obscure even while building lives have grown shorter. The refusal to accept building death, particularly the demise of important, influential, or historically valued buildings, has sometimes been an act of heroic resistance to short-sighted greed and insensitivity. At other times it has been an act of denial. It is one thing to oppose an apparently needless act of destruction that is costly on many levels. It is another to cling to the remains of the corpse from a misplaced sense of reverence or of guilt. In the past, when building lives were generally longer but, because cata-strophe was a perpetual threat, more uncertain, there was less reluc-tance to face up to disappearance. And less insistence upon perma-nence. When the first meeting house of a Boston congregation was

Demolition of Larkin
Building, Buffalo, 1950,
two views.

demolished in 1729, as the congregation prepared for larger quarters, a day of fasting and prayer was declared.[56] Architects themselves, seeing buildings age ungracefully, subject to humiliations from strangers, are often more willing than lay enthusiasts to accept death. In 1951, after years of neglect and deterioration, with dozens of broken windows, stripped lighting and plumbing fixtures, and partially dismantled sections, the forty-five-year-old Larkin Administration Building was demolished by authority of a permit from the city of Buffalo, which owned it. Although newspapers called the building a cadaver and a "spectacle of decay," its legendary status guaranteed special controversy. But by then even its architect, Frank Lloyd Wright, declared that it deserved a decent burial. It had served the purpose for which he intended it, Wright pointed out, and had already been subjected to many alterations he had

Cover drawing by Richter.

never approved. Wright complained that the Larkin owners had never properly appreciated his masterpiece anyway, in view of the changes they had made. What was wrong, then, with letting it go?[57]

But the continuing growth of architectural history as an academic discipline and of historic preservation as a popular pastime has given the corpses a new life. The technologies of photographic reproduction, and some newer computer-based methods, make it possible to commune with the dead. With a lengthy ancestry but in rapidly increasing numbers during the 1960s, a series of books appeared whose titles started with the word *Lost*. Once upon a time titles referring to lost places were dominated by explorations into ancient civilizations or exotic locales.[58] Now they referred to structures and life patterns barely a century old. Constance Greiff's *Lost America* of 1971, one of the early examples of the genre's new generation, had so many entries it was divided, using the Mississippi as a boundary, into two volumes.[59] By 1993 one could peruse *Lost New York, Lost Chicago, Lost Boston, Lost Toronto, Lost New Orleans, Lost Twin Cities,* and *Capital Losses,* along

View of Benjamin Franklin
Parkway from City Hall
Annex, Philadelphia,
c. 1930.

View of John F. Kennedy
Boulevard from City Hall
Annex, Philadelphia, 1987.
Photograph © Susan
Oyama.

with other books containing *Forgotten, Changing,* or *Remembered* in
their titles, and *Then and Now* photographic sequences juxtaposing
photographs of landscape tracts once rural and now urban or suburban, or once urban and now suburban or rural, separated by thirty,
fifty, or one hundred years.[60] Washington, D.C., Ithaca, New York City,
Pittsburgh, Philadelphia, and Seattle all have been subjects of *Then
and Now* volumes—sometimes, as in the case of Pittsburgh, celebrating the thrust of the transformation, but more often mourning the
ghosts of departed loved ones.[61] These sentiments were quite different
from the spirit of county and city histories that were published in great
numbers for fifty or sixty years following the Civil War. Illustrated

extensively, first with woodcuts and lithographs and only later with photographs, they too juxtaposed the present and past and made an occasional obeisance toward the loss of a cherished structure. But it was the new construction, the landscape interventions, and the economic growth that provided their heroic reason for being.

The appeal of the more recent texts, with their heavy reliance upon enlarged and expertly reprinted photographs, says something about the relation between photography and an interest in old or departed buildings, a relation that has much in common with the deep fascination photographs of the dead hold for so many people. In both genres the high degree of individuation residing within portraits of persons or specific places permits a sense of involvement. The authors of *Ithaca Then and Now* pay particular tribute to late-nineteenth-century architectural photographs as a prod to increased concern with our architectural heritage.[62] These pictures provide an opportunity for recognition and connection in ways that photographs of vanishing or vanished species, for example, do not. Clusters of specific buildings, photographed in their "before" or "lost" state, are analogous to representations of long-gone youth or dimly recalled relatives. They constitute an extended family album, one related to, but distinct from, the version described earlier, another device for establishing individual biography.

Such photographs also serve as instruments in the establishment of family trees, a genealogical pursuit which for many years has been a consuming passion of most architectural historians. Only the list of begats in the Bible exceeds the complex lineages presumed to govern individual structures. Not all of the paternity is legitimate, of course, but photographs and engravings, particularly of buildings as they once were, help to make the case.

Building lives, unlike the lives of human beings, have not stimulated the attention of many biographers. Certainly many great structures—cathedrals, royal palaces, Greek temples, mosques, some government buildings—have received book-length studies. Some buildings, indeed, have had several monographs devoted to them. For the most part such subjects constitute heroic and influential architectural expressions; biographers have concentrated on their structural and stylistic evolution. The commissioning of plans, the challenge of financing them, the character of changes and modifications sometimes executed over the course of many centuries, the participation of famous architects and designers, these have constituted the dominant thrust of such stories.[63] And tourist attractions have stimulated a range of more ephemeral if lavishly illustrated publications, some of

APRIL 18, 1906

SEPTEMBER 1937

Photos recording transformation of San Francisco Call Building, *Life*, August 8, 1938, p. 68.

DECEMBER 1937

JANUARY 1938

MARCH 1938

JUNE 1938

them concentrating on beheadings, murders, royal scandals, and seditious plots, newsworthy events that supply a human narrative.

But still more recently a new textual genre has begun to appear, particularly in this country. It represents something of a synthesis. While pride of place continues to be given those buildings viewed as important by reason of structural innovation or stylistic celebrity, the range of building types has been expanded to include far more commercial and industrial examples. And the sense of subject has been broadened to incorporate the work and business practices a building's spaces enclosed as well as the organizational culture it supported, the popular as well as professional reception given to its appearance, the circumstances leading to its demise, if it is no longer standing, the systems of adaptive reuse proposed for its survival, and similar matters. In the United States such studies now include Jack Quinan's book on the Larkin Building and Joseph Siry's on Carson Pirie Scott.[64] Further works are promised on other major structures. Building biography promises to become an effective forum for examining the eventfulness of both American buildings and the larger landscape. In due course it may become as standard a form as human biography.

And this may serve as a bridge to some remarks on the larger subject of the life rituals of constructed forms. In these three essays I have attempted to demonstrate that certain insights can be gained from the application of a life cycle metaphor to buildings, as well as from an inventory of the rituals attached to these life stages. Indeed, I have proposed that these ceremonies, along with our nomenclature and a series of other assumptions, reveal a broad tendency to conceive of buildings as lives. The need to establish the scope and variety of these rituals, as well as to demonstrate their broad application, may well have given many of my observations an apparently casual or episodic character. It seems now appropriate, even necessary, to try to suggest more systematically some of the uses that can be made of such analysis, the payback for more serious and comprehensive gathering of detail about building rites of passage. The broader objective here lies in mapping some additional routes for historians of inhabited structures to take, ways of linking their work with other, quite different research strategies. Why, then, should we pay attention to these apparently prosaic details that relate, in general, more to the financing, promotion, maintenance, social uses, and planning politics of architecture than to actual design and construction? Let me suggest three major reasons. The first, as a policy

metaphorically
city life

use. The second, as a phenomenological device. And the third, as a suggested ground for critical historiography.

First of all, examining buildings through their life stages and modes of representation encourages us to conceive of them not simply as places but as sets of events, affixing a temporal dimension to their existence that is not simply an add-on but fundamental to their nature.[65] Without venturing on to more complex philosophical terrain or invoking the language appropriate to such discussions, this involves acknowledging building personality without demanding that it stay permanently the same. The advantages of creating an event category for buildings seem multiple, particularly if we wish to penetrate the ideological significance of architectural form. Leaving aside this issue for a moment, there are major implications for preservationist positions as well. We require new and stronger arguments for the retention or adaptation of certain structures than the simple grounds of their having been around for a long time and our sentimental affection for them. The notion of structural lifetimes may provide part of a more persuasive strategy of evaluation, in considering when euthanasia is appropriate or not and why we need to salvage what no longer is the original personality or anything like it. We also need more effective mourning rituals for the buildings that are taken down. Despite our skill in documenting every aspect of their structure and appearance, providing a record for the future more detailed than that given most human beings, we have not done much in the way of preparing funeral services. The opportunity to eulogize a structure in its last days may be more significant than the need to pay promotional tribute to it in its first hours.

A second reason to think more about the implications of building rites of passage and life histories is our continuing need to understand objects by attributes that do not inherently belong to them. Concluding a recent essay, the anthropologist Marshall Sahlins invoked John Locke's *Essay Concerning Human Understanding* and its effort to promote a more relational knowledge of things. Objects can often be better understood from their relations to their neighbors than by abstract definitional categories. Sahlins notes the value of this viewpoint to anthropologists (and historians). After all, Sahlins argues, an object's very objectivity rests on "a historically relative selection and symbolic valuation of only some of the possible concrete referents."[66] Not only scholars make such selections. All cultural systems do so.

It is possible, of course, to examine buildings by any number of formal devices, to consider their orders, structure, systems of ornament, or material ingredients without much referencing to contextual history

yes

and culture. It has been so done for many centuries, as it has for many other subjects from medicine to archaeology. The internalist examination will remain of central importance, particularly to professionals who are the usual practitioners of the mysteries.

But the art of explaining how and why things look the way they do also compels the creation of a universe of referents that falls outside such categories. Or so it seems in our times. This art requires our examining the enabling circumstances and the individual resources of designer, builder, and patron. It means also talking about the social expectations entertained for certain kinds of structures, about the systems of imagery applied to translate and describe their physical appearance, about the status of buildings as new, middle-aged, old, or outworn. And it means understanding why we keep or try to keep certain structures unchanged, why we change and retain others, and why we dispense entirely with still others.

And this, in turn, opens up a third set of issues that revolve around the social understanding of buildings and architecture, the means by which people relate or do not relate to the built environment, how they talk or do not talk about it, what parts building style and structural scale play in our culture as a whole. It has been argued by a number of recent critics and theorists that architectural meaning inevitably reflects and legitimates power relationships and hegemonic patterns.[67] Indeed, such meaning seems so pervasive that neither parody nor opposition is an effective instrument of challenge. Revolutionary or even critical architecture, from this view, is impossible. How can cultural texts that are so naturalized in the dominant rhetoric serve in any way as sources of criticism? Must one turn to critical historians to demystify what practitioners themselves cannot, because constructed buildings contribute so powerfully to the mythification of social reality? If so, what are the materials that such critical historians can draw upon?

Again, it might be argued that the rituals of the building life cycle and the history of graphic representation constitute especially privileged instruments by which to translate into accessible experiences the social role of architecture. For these efforts, however fleeting, transient, and often conventionalized, can objectify the meanings attached to a structure's history, its sponsors, its functions, the aspirations lavished upon it. And their texture can reveal, by intention or not, the forces that gave these structures life. Lined up on either side of the steam shovel, surrounding the cornerstone, organizing the tours, or smiling through the pages of promotional brochures and commemorative histories are the godfathers and godmothers of the enterprises so publicized. And if backers and investors are not invariably pictured attending the obsequies as well, that is because the police are there also, as they might be visiting a gangster's funeral, looking to see who is in attendance. Great buildings are generally assumed to have been murdered; the idea of their dying a natural death seems unacceptable. In the absence of a reformed legal system, only historians are able to constitute a coroner's jury, to initiate an inquest.

I hope this trio of arguments, added to what has already been said, endorses the value of further study and more especially the gathering of data about the life patterns of buildings. Changing patterns of ritualization are often revelations of shifting values and expectations. And differing patterns, in different places, highlight the varieties of cultural experience. The elements for this, the stories, the folklore and ceremonies and procedures, lie all around us, so numerous, so trivialized, so repetitive that they have narcotized us about their larger meaning. But they constitute a part of the life of buildings. And they should play their part in future narratives, as they have played their signifying role for many centuries. Their scholarly recovery and deployment should reflect the larger direction of an effort already under way, vivifying many of the details of daily experience and assigning them a place within a rich medley of comparative cultural practices. Building lives and rites of passage are part of our inherited way of organizing the physical world, devices that acknowledge the importance of the built environment and the need to respond to the call of the sacred. The textual recovery of these practices constitutes both a challenge to writers of architectural history and a promise of a new way of relating to the heritage that surrounds us all.

Is arch. history really this old school? a call for interdis. seems so old, dated, dull by this point

Notes

Introduction

1. Suzanne Preston Blier, "Houses are human: Architectural self-images of Africa's Taberma," *Journal of the Society of Architectural Historians* 14 (December 1983), 371–382.

2. Gelett Burgess, *The lively city o' Ligg: A cycle of modern fairy tales for city children* (New York: Stokes, 1899), 26.

1. Meeting the World

1. Joseph Rykwert, *The idea of a town: The anthropology of urban form in Rome, Italy, and the ancient world* (Princeton: Princeton University Press, 1976), 174.

2. Jonathan Z. Smith, *To take place: Toward theory in ritual* (Chicago: University of Chicago Press, 1987), distinguishes among the place-consciousness of various religions and argues that it might be possible to locate "any particular building ideology along a continuum from the sphere of 'nature' to that of 'culture'" (21). Although most Indo-European buildings terms, argues Smith, are "relentlessly social," Indian temples can be considered to have "grown" from seeds. In the Near East "a temple is built where it happens to have been built." Its function is royal, its position more arbitrary.

3. Rykwert provides expert comparative guidance. In his extraordinarily learned and complex book Rykwert admits his concern had been "to show the town as a total mnemonic symbol, or at any rate a structured complex of symbols; in which the citizen, through a number of bodily exercises, such as processions, seasonal festivals, sacrifices, identifies himself with his town, with its past and its founders." Rykwert, *Idea of a town*, 189.

4. For feng shui see, among dozens of texts, Sarah Rossbach, *Feng shui: The Chinese art of placement* (New York: Penguin Arkana, 1983, 1991).

5. The current appeal of these rituals is evidenced by numerous magazine and newspaper articles. See, for example, Ashley Dunn, "Ancient Chinese craft reshaping building design and sales in U.S.," *New York Times*, Sept. 22, 1994; Nicholas D. Kristof, "In a computer age, Shinto devils still prowl," *New York Times*, Oct. 15, 1995; and Molly O'Neill, "Feng shui or feng phooey?" *New York Times*, Jan. 9, 1997.

6. Herbert L. Kessler, "On the state of medieval art history," *Art Bulletin* 70 (June 1988), 174.

7. Marchita B. Mauck, "The mosaic of the triumphal arch of S. Prassede: A liturgical interpretation," *Speculum* 62 (1987), 814.

8. See, for example, Nicolai Rubinstein, "Vasari's painting of *The Foundation of Florence* in the Palazzo Vecchio," in Douglas Fraser et al., eds., *Essays in the history of architecture presented to Rudolf Wittkower* (London: Phaidon, 1967), 64–73.

9. E. C. Harrington, *The object, impor-*

tance, and antiquity of the rite of consecration of churches...(London: Rivington, 1844), 4.

10. Patrick J. Geary, *Furta sacra: Thefts of relics in the central Middle Ages* (Princeton: Princeton University Press, 1978); and Patrick J. Geary, "Sacred commodities: The circulation of medieval relics," in Arjun Appadurai, ed., *The social life of things: Commodities in cultural perspective* (Cambridge: Cambridge University Press, 1992), 169–191. This essay was originally published in 1986.

11. Peter W. Williams, "The medieval heritage in American religious architecture," in Bernard Rosenthal and Paul E. Szarmach, eds., *Medievalism in American culture* (Binghamton, N.Y.: Medieval and Renaissance Texts and Studies, 1989), 172.

12. Peter Brown, *The cult of the saints: Its rise and function in Latin Christianity* (Chicago: University of Chicago Press, 1981), 88. See also Barbara Fay Abou-El-Haj, *The medieval cult of saints: Formations and transformations* (Cambridge: Cambridge University Press, 1994).

13. See, among others, Lee Bowen, "The tropology of mediaeval dedication rites," *Speculum* 16 (October 1941), 469–479; Donald J. Sheerin, "Dedication of churches," in Joseph R. Strayer, ed., *Dictionary of the Middle Ages* (New York: Scribner, 1984), 130–131.

14. For more on the history of christenings and launchings see Fletcher S. Bassett, *Sea phantoms; or legends and superstitions of the sea and of sailors in all lands and at all times* (Chicago: Morrill, Higgins, 1885, 1892); and William J. Baxter, "Launching cruisers and battleships," *Scribner's* 12 (October 1892), 488–499.

15. Bowen, "Tropology of mediaeval dedication rites," describes the elaborate symbolism of church consecration.

16. *The form and order of the service...at the consecration of the cathedral church of*

Saint Michael, Coventry (Cambridge: Cambridge University Press, 1962), contains a useful summary of consecration rites and a discussion of the key delivery ceremony, 1–2.

17. For more on various kinds of dedication ceremonies for one cathedral see Chr. Wordsworth, ed., *Ceremonies and processions of the cathedral church of Salisbury* (Cambridge: Cambridge University Press, 1901).

18. Marchita Mauck suggests that the dedication date of July 20 may have been selected by Pope Paschal I as part of his continuing effort to identify himself with Constantine. See Mauck, "Mosaic of the triumphal arch," 828.

19. This and many other complex procedures are treated by J. Wickham Legg, ed., *English orders for consecrating churches in the seventeenth century* (London: Harrison, 1911). This is volume 41 of the Henry Bradshaw Society, an organization founded to edit liturgical texts.

20. Thus the consecration of Troyes Cathedral, July 9, 1430, was decided upon by Bishop Jean Leguise not because of the construction achieved but to celebrate the expulsion of the Anglo-Burgundians from the city and reaffirm the loyalty of the bishop and his chapter to the royal house. See Stephen Murray, *Building Troyes Cathedral: The late Gothic campaigns* (Bloomington: Indiana University Press, 1987), 46. Nave, tower, and choir collapses had complicated the lengthy building project. Gloucester Cathedral was dedicated in 1100, but there is doubt as to how much of the building was actually completed by this date. David Welander suggests that in many churches of the period, dedication might take place as soon as the monks could actually use the presbytery and liturgical choir. See David Welander, *The history, art, and architecture of Gloucester Cathedral* (Wolfeboro Falls, N.H.: Alan Sutton, 1991). Canterbury Cathedral was consecrated in 1077, con-

sisting only of the choir, transept, and a few bays of the nave. Francis Woodman, *The architectural history of Canterbury Cathedral* (London: Routledge and Kegan Paul, 1981), 28.

21. See Marcia B. Hall, *Renovation and counter-reformation: Vasari and Duke Cosimo in Sta Maria Novella and Sta Croce, 1565–1577* (Oxford: Clarendon, 1979). Decrees of the Council of Trent established procedures by which bishops could exercise new controls over church renovations and the placement of images. Many Catholics considered church designs and liturgical practices to be out of step with social needs, objecting in particular to the physical barriers, such as immense rood-screens and choir enclosures, which separated clergy from lay people.

22. Marian Card Donnelly, *The New England meeting houses of the seventeenth century* (Middletown, Conn.: Wesleyan University Press, 1968), points out the tradition of using English parish churches as assembly halls, schools, or markets. Her careful study of the building type makes little reference to dedication or consecration ceremonies, although she notes that the 1699 dedication of Boston's Brattle Street Church, the earliest known church with tower and spire at one end, featured a Biblical passage suggesting "the sanctity of the building, which the Puritans had denied" (79).

23. Peter Benes and Philip D. Zimmerman, *New England meeting house and church: 1630–1850* (Boston: Boston University and Currier Gallery, 1979), 2.

24. See, for example, Reverend A. N. Somers, *History of Lancaster, New Hampshire* (Concord: Rumford, 1899), 204–206, who provides an elaborate and evocative description of building raisings.

25. Allen Johnson, ed., *Dictionary of American biography* (New York: Scribner's, 1928), I, 319.

26. For more on Freemasony in this period see James Stevens Curl, *The art and architecture of Freemasonry: An introduc-*
tory study (London: Batsford, 1991); Lynn Dumenil, *Freemasonry and American culture, 1880–1930* (Princeton: Princeton University Press, 1984); Margaret C. Jacob, *Living the enlightenment: Freemasonry and politics in eighteenth-century Europe* (New York: Oxford University Press, 1991); and Dorothy Ann Lipson, *Freemasonry in federalist Connecticut* (Princeton: Princeton University Press, 1977).

27. See particularly Steven C. Bullock, *Revolutionary brotherhood: Freemasonry and the transformation of the American social order, 1730–1840* (Chapel Hill: University of North Carolina Press, 1996).

28. An exception is Bullock, *Revolutionary brotherhood*. While not devoting a great deal of space to the cornerstone rituals, Bullock describes several, noting the great variety of structures the Masons dedicated and remarking that "the American ceremonies were part of a self-conscious attempt to create new images that could celebrate and inculcate Revolutionary ideals" (150).

29. C. Lance Brockman, *Theatre of the fraternity: Staging the ritual space of the Scottish Rite of Freemasonry, 1896–1929* (Minneapolis: Frederick R. Weisman Art Museum; Jackson: University Press of Mississippi, 1996), contains essays and illustrations exploring various aspects of Masonic ceremonialism.

30. For a review of Masonic cornerstone laying and building rituals see Ray Baker Harris, *The laying of cornerstones: Freemasonry's part in preserving the practice of one of the world's most ancient customs* (Washington, D.C.: Supreme Council 33 Ancient and Accepted Scottish Rite, 1961).

31. Lipson, *Freemasonry in federalist Connecticut*, 318. Colden himself was the author of a memoir, commissioned by the New York Common Council, recounting the extraordinary ceremonies associated with the opening of the Erie Canal, a level of pageantry that he presumably enjoyed.

32. For Lafayette's role as a layer of corner-stones and for Masonic building pageantry in this era see Marc H. Miller, "Lafayette's farewell tour and American art," in Stanley Idzerda et al., *Lafayette, hero of two worlds* (Hanover, N.H.: Queens Museum and University Press of New England, 1989), 91–109. Lafayette laid cornerstones for, among other things, the Bunker Hill Monument, the monument for General Nathaniel Greene, and the memorial for General Count Pulaski.

33. Dumenil, *Freemasonry and American culture*, 235.

34. Only rarely was the propriety of Masonic ceremonies and symbols mingling with public buildings questioned. For a few such controversies see Marian M. Ohman, *Missouri's courthouses* (Columbia: University of Missouri Press, 1983), 109–118.

35. The regalia employed by Masons on such occasions have formed the basis for collection and exhibition. See, for example, Barbara Franco, *Bespangled, painted, and embroidered: Decorated Masonic aprons in America, 1790–1850* (Lexington, Mass.: Scottish Rite Masonic Museum of Our National Heritage, 1980).

36. Edward Norman, *The house of God: Church architecture, style, and history* (London: Thames and Hudson, 1990), 237.

37. J. R. Hale, "The end of Florentine liberty: The Fortezza da Basso," in Nicolai Rubinstein, ed., *Florentine studies: Politics and society in Renaissance Florence* (Evanston: Northwestern University Press, 1968), 501–532.

38. Harris, *Laying of cornerstones*, argues that the first record of a formal, official Masonic cornerstone laying in Scotland dates the event to 1738, not many years after the ceremonies were developed in England.

39. Wayne A. Huss, *The master builders: A history of the Grand Lodge of Free and Accepted Masons of Pennsylvania* (Philadelphia: Grand Lodge F. and A. M. of Pennsylvania, 1986), reviews the elaborate symbolism of the ceremonies, particularly with regard to the construction of lodge halls.

40. The whiskey bottle was inserted in the cornerstone of the Coryell County Courthouse. See Willard B. Robinson and Todd Webb, *Texas public buildings of the nineteenth century* (Austin: Amon Carter Museum of Western Art, University of Texas Press, 1974).

41. Time capsules were closely associated with American world's fairs and were meant to withstand the ravages of centuries. When, occasionally, one was opened after only decades of burials, the contents were found to have faded or crumbled. See "The Talk of the Town. Postscript," *New Yorker* 39 (June 29, 1963), 18–19, for one such instance. For the hubris associated with the sinking of time capsules see *The book of record of the time capsule of Cupaloy deemed capable of resisting the effect of time for five thousand years preserving an account of universal achievements embedded in the grounds of the New York World's Fair, 1939* (New York: Westinghouse, 1938). For more on time capsule thinking see "Remains to be seen," *Newsweek* 64 (Sept. 28, 1964), 92.

42. George Dallas Albert, ed., *History of the county of Westmoreland, Pennsylvania* (Philadelphia: Everts, 1882), 426.

43. James W. Savage and John T. Bell, *History of the city of Omaha, Nebraska* (New York: Munsell, 1894), 217.

44. See, for example, Franklin P. Rice, ed., *The Worcester of 1898* (Worcester: Blanchard, 1899), 89; Col. Frederick L. Hitchcock, *History of Scranton and its people* (New York: Lewis, 1914), I, 269; A. J. Weise, *History of the city of Troy* (Troy: Young, 1876), 155–156. Weise's text indicated that for the 1827 cornerstone laying of Saint Paul's Church in Troy, New York, a silver plate on which was engraved the narration of the cornerstone laying was inserted, along with various other items, into the cornerstone itself.

45. Glenn Brown, *History of the United States Capitol* (Washington: Government Printing Office, 1900; New York: Da Capo, 1970), 121.

46. One classic version of this ceremony was the September 1793 cornerstone laying for the U.S. Capitol, presided over by George Washington, wearing a sash and apron presented to him by the wife of the Marquis de Lafayette. See Brown, *History of the Capitol*, 14–16. A full description of such ceremonies can be found in many places, but a particularly detailed account is in Rice, *The Worcester of 1898*, 83–118.

47. "The Cathedral corner-stone," *Harper's Weekly* 37 (Jan. 7, 1893), 7.

48. For a full description see *Proceedings at the reception and dinner in honor of George Peabody, Esq.* . . . (Boston: Dutton, 1856).

49. For a typical late-nineteenth-century example see Jane Durrell, "Centennial of the dedication of the Cincinnati Art Museum's original building, May 17, 1886," *Queen City Heritage* 44 (Spring 1986), 30–36, which features a description of the event. Five thousand people attended, entering a rotunda filed with ferns and flowers and listening to a concert that ended with a Mendelssohn chorus.

50. The 1904 dedication of Chicago's Orchestra Hall featured a typical program. It began with "Hail Bright Abode," an aria from Richard Wagner's *Tannhäuser,* and was followed by the overture to that opera, Richard Strauss's *Death and Transfiguration,* Beethoven's Fifth Symphony, and Handel's Hallelujah Chorus. A special commemorative program was printed, *Orchestra Hall: Dedication, Wednesday, December 14, 1904.* More than ninety years later, the Wagner aria remained popular, reopening the restored and renovated San Francisco Opera House. See Anthony Tommasini, "Golden opera house glitters anew," *New York Times,* Oct. 8, 1997.

51. Huss, *Master builders.* The cost of this

new temple was more than 1.5 million dollars. For New York see "The new Masonic Temple," *Harper's Weekly* 14 (June 25, 1870), 404.

52. See, for example, *Exercises at the opening of the James Blackstone Memorial Library, Branford, Connecticut, June 17, 1896* (New Haven: Tuttle, Morehouse, and Taylor, 1897).

53. Alan W. Ball, *The public libraries of greater London: A pictorial history, 1856–1914* (London: Library Association, 1977), contains separate chapters on stone-laying ceremonies and opening ceremonies, rich in illustrated examples.

54. For more information on the history of wrapping see Thomas Hine, *The total package: The evolution and secret meanings of boxes, bottles, cans, and tubes* (Boston: Little, Brown, 1995); and Alec Davis, *Package and print: The development of container and label design* (New York: Clarkson N. Potter, 1968).

55. "The statue habit," *Nation* 97 (July 17, 1913), 50.

56. "The designing of monuments," *American Architect and Building News* 1 (Aug. 18, 1877), 262.

57. For contemporary descriptions see, among others, *Proceedings upon the unveiling of the statue of Baron von Steuben* (Washington: United States Congress, 1912); John Spargo, *The Bennington battle monument: Its story and its meaning* (Rutland, Vt.: Tuttle, 1925); June Hargrove, "Unveiling the Colossus," in Pierre Provoyeur and June Hargrove, eds., *Liberty: The French-American statue in art and history* (Cambridge: Harper and Row Perennial Library, 1986), 198–202.

58. "The Benton statue," *Harper's Weekly* 12 (June 20, 1868), 398. For more descriptions of statuary unveilings see Burke Wilkinson, *Uncommon clay: The life and works of Augustus Saint-Gaudens* (San Diego: Harcourt Brace Jovanovich, 1985); Kathy Edward, Esme Howard, and Toni Prawl, *Monument Avenue: History and architecture* (Washington:

Historic American Buildings Survey, 1992); and Penny Balkin Bach, *Public art in Philadelphia* (Philadelphia: Temple University Press, 1992), 62–70.

59. Several of these are described in some detail in David E. Nye, *American technological sublime* (Cambridge: MIT Press, 1994), chaps. 3–4.

60. John Seelye, *Beautiful machine: Rivers and the republican plan, 1755–1825* (New York: Oxford University Press, 1991), 291–374, describes various public celebrations of the period, notably the Erie Canal opening of 1825. For a contemporary description see Cadwallader D. Colden, *Memoir, prepared at the request of a committee of the common council of the city of New York . . . at the celebration of the completion of the New York Canals* (New York: Corporation of New York, 1825).

61. Alan Trachtenberg, *Brooklyn Bridge: Fact and symbol,* 2d edition (Chicago: University of Chicago Press, 1979), remains the authoritative study of this landmark event. See particularly chap. 7, "Opening ceremonies," 115–127. See also *The great East River Bridge, 1883–1983* (Brooklyn: Harry N. Abrams for the Brooklyn Museum, 1983). For another great bridge opening see Edward Hungerford, *The Williamsburg Bridge: An account of the ceremonies attending the formal opening of the structure* (Brooklyn: Eagle Press, 1903). For bridge pageants of an earlier day see Wilbur J. Watson and Sara Ruth Watson, *Bridges in history and legend* (Cleveland: Jansen, 1937), chap. 6.

62. For references to many such events see, among a number of other texts, Alvin F. Harlow, *The road of the century: The story of the New York Central* (New York: Creative Age Press, 1947).

63. See Edward Hungerford, *The story of the Baltimore and Ohio Railroad, 1827–1927* (New York: G. P. Putnam's, 1928), especially 1: 37–47, 171–173; and Jancy Goyne Evans, "History on a bandbox: A pictorial record of the founding of the Baltimore and Ohio Railroad,"

Winterthur Portfolio 5 (1969), 123–128.

64. Another notable railroad completion was the 1853 arrival of the Baltimore and Ohio Railroad in Wheeling. For a detailed description of the event see James D. Dilts, *The great road: The building of the Baltimore and Ohio, the nation's first railroad, 1828–1853* (Stanford: Stanford University Press, 1993), chap. 25.

65. Theodore James, Jr., *The Empire State Building* (New York: Harper and Row, 1975), 63.

66. William Collins, "Our queerest building custom," *Pencil Points* 12 (March 1931), 179–182.

67. Mike Cherry, *On high steel: The education of an ironworker* (New York: Quadrangle/New York Times Press, 1974), 201.

68. For one description of a topping out see Karl Sarbagh, *Skyscraper: The making of a building* (London: Macmillan, Viking Penguin, 1989), 309–315.

69. Jerry Adler, *High rise* (New York: HarperCollins, 1993), 322. Adler relates, sometimes cynically, the complex process through which a New York high-rise structure is planned, financed, built, and leased.

70. The opening is described in many places, but for the most detailed description see *Dedicatory and opening ceremonies of the World's Columbian Exposition* (Chicago: Stone, Kastler, and Painter, 1893).

71. H. D. Northrup, *The world's fair as seen in one hundred days* (Philadelphia, 1893), 161.

72. James, *Empire State Building,* has more on the day's opening ceremonies.

73. Stephen Cassady, *Spanning the gate: The Golden Gate Bridge* (Mill Valley, Calif.: Squarebooks, 1986), treats the opening ceremonies for this bridge.

74. The richest and most suggestive commentaries here are Clare Cooper, *The house as symbol of self* (Berkeley: Institute of Urban and Regional Development, 1971), Working Paper 120. See also Abdelhalim Ibrahim

Abdelhalim, "The building ceremony," Ph.D. diss., University of California, Berkeley, 1987.

75. See the article "Mezuzah," in *Encyclopaedia Judaica*, (Jerusalem: Encyclopaedia Judaica, and New York: Macmillan, 1971), 11, 1474–1477.

76. Jack Quinan, *Frank Lloyd Wright's Larkin Building: Myth and fact* (Cambridge: MIT Press, 1987), 96. Quinan details the elaborate program of inspiration and indoctrination Wright and the Larkin Company produced. There was a long tradition of didactive inscriptions in public buildings as well, well established by the fourteenth century. See Nicolai Rubinstein, *The Palazzo Vecchio, 1298–1532* (Oxford: Clarendon, 1995), 49–52, 73–78.

77. Rykwert, *Idea of a town*, 40.

78. For some Italian practices and American contrasts, see Adria Bermondi, *Houses with names: The Italian immigrants of Highwood, Illinois* (Urbana: University of Illinois Press, 1990), 9. For other comments on European traditions see Gottfried Keller, "Names in Goldach," *Names* 1 (September 1953), 205–207; and Delia H. Pugh, "House and farm names in north Wales," *Names* 2 (March 1954), 28–30.

79. There are exceptions. The Alan Garage on New York's East Side was apparently named for the owner's first grandson, while an adjoining hotel was named for the boy's younger brother. See Christopher Gray, *Changing New York: The architectural scene* (New York: Dover, 1992), 87.

80. Some of the complications of corporate building names are explored in Rick Hampson, "Skyscraper name games often end in confusion," *Chicago Tribune*, Apr. 4, 1993.

81. Not always. Some cities are playing with the notion of renaming streets and parks for corporate sponsors. See Peter Applebome, "Adman in Atlanta tries to sell city," *New York Times*, Feb. 9, 1993.

82. William Ganson Rose, *Cleveland: The making of a city* (Cleveland: World, 1950), 787.

83. Jno. Gilmer Speed, "Naming apartment-houses," *Harper's Weekly* 38 (Mar. 24, 1894), 283. For typical names given turn of century New York apartment houses see G. C. Hesselgren, *Apartment houses of the metropolis* (New York: Hesselgren, 1908). For further analysis see Arthur Minton, "Apartment-house names," *American Speech* 20 (October 1945), 168–177. See also Elizabeth Collins Cromley, *Alone together: A history of New York's early apartments* (Ithaca: Cornell University Press, 1990), 142–143. "Usually the grander the name, the less pretentious the apartment house," notes James M. Goode, *Best addresses: A century of Washington's distinguished apartment houses* (Washington: Smithsonian Institution Press, 1988), 190.

84. See *The Apartment House* 2 (March 1912), 29. See also "Want a name for your new apartment house?" *The Apartment House* 2 (February 1912), 30.

85. See, for example, Arthur Minton, "Names of real-estate developments," parts I and II, *Names* 7 (1959), 129–153, 233–255.

86. See, for example, Karen Koegler, "A farewell to arms: The 'greening' of American apartment names," *Names* 34 (1986), 48–61.

87. For more on hotel names see James Algeo, "Hostelry names: The generics," *Mississippi Folklore Register* 11 (1977), 151–163.

2. Signs of Life

1. See Donnie Radcliffe, "White House buries times capsule," *Washington Post*, Oct. 14, 1992.

2. This was the experience of the University of Montana, preparing to celebrate its centennial. See *Chronicle of Higher Education*, Aug. 4, 1993, reprinted in *Chicago Maroon*, Aug. 6, 1993.

3. Hundreds of examples can be found in the Morris Fishbein Collection of birth

announcements, Special Collections, Joseph Regenstein Library, University of Chicago. This collection, which includes announcements originating in the 1920s, 1930s, and 1940s, remained uncollated in 1997 but held rich possibilities for social analysts.

4. Historians of photography have studied such things. See, among others, Julia Hirsch, *Family photographs: Content, meaning, and effect* (New York: Oxford University Press, 1981); Heinz K. Henisch and Bridget A. Henisch, *The photographic experience, 1839–1914: Images and attitudes* (University Park: Pennsylvania State University Press, 1994), chap. 6, "Family milestones," 165–196.

5. William Havard Eliot, *A description of Tremont house, with architectural illustrations* (Boston: Gray and Bowen, 1830).

6. See a summary of these trends in Ann Payne, *Views of the past: Topographical drawings in the British Library* (London: British Library, 1987).

7. For the work of Ackermann, and other notable aquatint productions of the early nineteenth century, see Martin Hardie, *English coloured books* (London, 1906), chap. 10, "Rudolph Ackermann."

8. *The Public Ledger Building, Philadelphia . . .* (Philadelphia: George W. Childs, 1868).

9. *Public Ledger Building*, 16.

10. See, for example, William H. Wheildon, *Memoir of Solomon Willard, architect and superintendent of the Bunker Hill Monument* (Boston: Monument Association, 1865); and, slightly later, George Washington Warren, *The history of the Bunker Hill Monument Association* (Boston: J. R. Osgood, 1877).

11. For example, *Description of Frazee's design for the Washington Monument, now exhibiting . . .* (New York: Jared W. Bell, 1848).

12. The only modern discussion I have found is a brief commentary in an exhibition catalogue, *Architectural brochures: History, hype, and graphic design* (Pittsburgh: Hunt Library, Carnegie-Mellon University, 1990). The earliest brochures included here are turn of the century, and there is some emphasis on recent architect-produced marketing materials. The building brochure is described by J. Lincoln Steffens, "The modern business building," *Scribner's Magazine* 22 (July 1897), 59.

13. *The Equitable Building* (New York: Equitable Office Building Corporation, 1914). This brochure measured forty-one centimeters in height, mimicking the great scale of its building.

14. William I. Garren, "Impressions," *Four Fifty Sutter Medical Building and the San Francisco Stock Exchange* (San Francisco: n.p., n.d.), 4.

15. Edwin A. Cochran, *The cathedral of commerce* (New York: Broadway Park Place Co., 1917), 6.

16. For the Woolworth Building see also *The master builders: A record of the world's highest commercial structure* (New York: H. McAlanney, 1913).

17. See, for example, *The Metropolitan Life Insurance Company* (New York: Metropolitan Life, 1908); *Union Arcade Building* (Pittsburgh, 1916); *Illinois Merchants Bank Buildings* (Chicago: Illinois Trust Safety Deposit Company, 1922); *The Prudential building, opened A.D. 1891* (Newark: Prudential Printing, 1891); *Equitable Building* (New York: Equitable Office Building Corporation, 1914).

18. For more on these pattern books, and a careful survey of their influence in one state, see Robert P. Guter and Janet W. Foster, *Building by the book: Pattern-book architecture in New Jersey* (New Brunswick: Rutgers University Press, 1992). See also Gwendolyn Wright, *Moralism and the model home: Domestic architecture and culture conflict in Chicago, 1873–1913* (Chicago: University of Chicago Press, 1980).

19. Edward R. Tufte, *The visual display of quantitative information* (Cheshire, Conn.: Graphics, 1983); and Edward R.

Tufte, *Envisioning information* (Cheshire, Conn.: Graphics, 1990).

20. The architect quoted was the Philadelphian Benjamin Linfoot, in James F. O'Gorman, "The Philadelphia architectural drawing in its historical context: An overview," in James F. O'Gorman et al., *Drawing toward building: Philadelphia architectural graphics, 1732–1986* (Philadelphia: University of Pennsylvania Press, 1986), 8.

21. Samuel Swift, "The pictorial representation of architecture: The work of Jules Guerin," *Brickbuilder* 18 (September 1909), 177.

22. For more on the larger subject see David Gebhard and Deborah Nevins, *200 years of American architectural drawings* (New York: Watson-Guptill, 1977); and Deborah Nevins and Robert A. M. Stern, *The architect's eye: American architectural drawings from 1799–1978* (New York: Pantheon, 1979).

23. Reproductions of this generation of renderers can be found in Arthur L. Guptill, *Color in sketching and rendering* (New York: Reinhold, 1935). Most of this work had appeared in the journal *Pencil Points* during the previous fifteen years. *Brickbuilder* 23 (1914) ran, in monthly issues, eleven articles in a series, "Monographs on architectural renderings," featuring artists like Alfred Githens, Rockwell Kent, and others.

24. For Ferriss see Hugh Ferriss, *The metropolis of tomorrow* (New York: Washburn, 1929); and Hugh Ferriss, *Power in buildings: An artist's view of contemporary architecture* (New York: Columbia University Press, 1953). *Power in buildings* includes sketches done for architects and developers in previous years.

25. Certain printers, like Chicago's R. R. Donnelley, made a specialty of such lavish brochures. Among the most impressive work they produced was *20 North Wacker Drive: A 42-story business structure in the heart of central Chicago* (Chicago: Lakeside, 1929?); *The Field*

Building* (Chicago: n.p., 1934); *The Chicago Stadium* (Chicago, 1928); and *The colossus of market places: The Merchandise Mart* (Chicago: n.p., n.d.). Will Howell & Associates, a local firm, designed several of these brochures, and various illustrators and photographers, some with wider reputations, like Egbert Jacobson and Hedrich-Blessing, worked on the details. *Rockefeller Center* (New York: Rockefeller Center, 1932), with John Wenrich renderings, and *The Fisher Building* (Detroit: New Center Development Corporation, n.d.), with illuminated initials and elegant color illustrations, are other notable examples.

26. It might be noted that the building books were paralleled by the appearance of hundreds of pamphlets, books, and brochures containing proposals for reforms in city planning. See the references and discussion of this rich graphic tradition in Neil Harris, "Graphic art for the public welfare," *Graphic design in America: A visual language history* (Minneapolis: Walker Art Center and Abrams, 1989), particularly 87–92.

27. A typical list of these suppliers can be found in the elegant *History of the Peoples Gas Building construction: Its progress from foundation to flag pole* (Chicago: D. H. Burnham, 1911).

28. One elaborate British text, sporting an embossed cover, featured *The new Cunard building* (Liverpool: Taylor, Garnett, Evans, and Company, 1917).

29. See Eve Blau and Edward Kaufman, eds., *Architecture and its image: Four centuries of architectural representation* (Montreal: Centre Canadien d'Architecture, 1989), for discussions of the photographic albums recording the construction of the Forth Bridge. Mary J. Shapiro, *A picture history of the Brooklyn Bridge with 107 prints and photographs* (New York: Dover, 1985), contains a description of photographs commissioned during the construction of that great project. Henri Loyrette, *Gustave Eiffel* (New York: Rizzoli, 1985),

reproduces photographs documenting the construction of the Eiffel Tower, as well as other Eiffel works. Finally, see the section "Construction and progress" in Robert A. Sobieszek, *"This edifice is colossal": 19th-century architectural photography* (Rochester: Rochester International Museum of Photography at George Eastman House, 1986). For more on the culture of construction in the nineteenth century see Tom F. Peters, *Building the nineteenth century* (Cambridge: MIT Press, 1996).

30. Cervin Robinson and Joel Herschman, *Architecture transformed: A history of the photography of buildings from 1839 to the present* (New York: Architectural League of New York; Cambridge: MIT Press, 1987), 43, 47, 52, discusses the appearance of photographic albums that reveal the progress of the building of the South Kensington Museum and London's 1862 Exposition. For a discussion of the creation of such photographic series, which included other notable structures like the Paris Opera, see Ulrich Keller, *The building of the Panama Canal in historic photographs* (New York: Dover, 1983), especially vii–ix.

31. O. F. Semsch, ed., *A history of the Singer Building construction: Its progress from foundation to flag pole* (New York: Shumway and Beattie, 1908).

32. See Blau and Kaufman, *Architecture and its image*, 270–281.

33. See Richard W. Unger, *The art of medieval technology: Images of Noah the shipbuilder* (New Brunswick: Rutgers University Press, 1991); and Andrea Louise Matthies, "Perceptions of technological change: Medieval artists view building construction," Ph.D. diss., State University of New York, Binghamton, 1984. *Der traum von raum: Gemalte architektur aus 7 jahrhunderten* (Marburg: Wolfram Hitzeroth, 1986), an exhibition catalogue for a show in Nuremberg, contains eighteen essays on painters' interpretations of architecture and architectural construc-

tion, including the building of the Tower of Babel.

34. One example of the interest in construction drawings can be found in Joseph Pennell, *Joseph Pennell's pictures of the wonder of work* (Philadelphia: Lippincott, 1916), a collection of drawings, etchings, and lithographs, including construction studies, prepared over a thirty-five-year period. Artists contemporaneous with Pennell were also absorbed by construction as a subject. One of them, W. B. Van Ingen, was noted for his Panama Canal studies, another, the Impressionist Childe Hassam, for skyscraper construction. Other depicters of construction in America included White, Colin Cooper, J. Alden Weir, and George Bellows. Pennell's illustrations included bridge- and shipbuilding, public building works, and construction of the Woolworth building, among many others. For Bellows see Marianne Doezema, *George Bellows and urban America* (New Haven: Yale University Press, 1992), chap. 1, "The excavation," 9–66, which discusses Bellows's four paintings of the Pennsylvania Station excavation process in Manhattan. Doezema also reproduces a number of the L. H. Dreyer photographs, which chronicled the progress of construction at regular intervals.

35. Builders themselves eventually served spectatorial interest in construction by demarcating areas for the "sidewalk superintendents" to watch. It is unclear how far back the custom goes, but claims have been made for Rockefeller Center's priority. Supposedly John D. Rockefeller, Jr., ordered portholes to be made in the fence surrounding the site. The source, "The talk of the town," *New Yorker* 32 (June 2, 1956), 23, was cited in the "Sidewalk superintendents" entry in B. A. Botkin, ed., *New York City folklore: Legends, tall tales, anecdotes, stories, sagas, heroes and characters, customs, traditions, and sayings* (New York: Random House, 1956), 438. Builders had, much

earlier, fenced off areas and sometimes constructed sheds over surrounding sidewalks for the safety of the public. See Arnold Lewis, *An early encounter with tomorrow: Europeans, Chicago's Loop, and the World's Columbian Exposition* (Urbana: University of Illinois Press, 1997), 38–40.

36. Edward Hungerford, *The Williamsburg Bridge: An account of the ceremonies attending the formal opening of the structure, December the nineteenth, MDCC-CCIII* (Brooklyn: Eagle Press, 1903).

37. Among the varieties see, for example, the photographs for Francis H. Kimball, "The construction of a great building," *Engineering Magazine* 8 (February 1895), 877–892; and Eadweard Muybridge's work for the building of the San Francisco Mint. See also William A. Bullough, "Eadweard Muybridge and the old San Francisco Mint: Archival photographs as historical documents," *California History* 68 (Spring–Summer 1989), 2–13.

38. Lewis W. Hine, *Men at work: Photographic studies of modern men and machines* (New York: Macmillan, 1932). Another elaborate text on the construction of the Empire State Building was prepared by the artist, Vernon Howe Bailey, for the builders, the Starrett Company, and issued in elephant folio size: Vernon Howe Bailey, *Empire State: A pictorial record of its construction* (New York: William Edwin Rudge, 1931). It is noteworthy that children's photographic books multiplied in the 1930s as well, books on technology, machines, animals, and construction, among them Elsa H. Naumburg, Clare Lambert, and Lucy Sprague Mitchell, *Skyscraper* (New York: John Day, 1932), a book based on Hine's photographs. See Barbara Bader, *American picturebooks from Noah's ark to the beast within* (New York: Collier-Macmillan, 1976), 100–117.

39. See Carol E. Roark et al., eds., *Catalogue of the Amon Carter Museum Photography Collection* (Fort Worth: Amon Carter Museum, 1993), 456–457.

40. See the panelist comment at a conference on the press and city building, "Press given critical role in urban change," *Editor and Publisher* 95 (Oct. 13, 1962), 13. But architects and critics were not always sure that omitting authorship was bad. Percy Cashmore, "What's in a name?" *Pencil Points* 10 (April 1929), 245, argued that a building's authors included not only its designers but its contractors, its builders, and a host of other people. They were too numerous for listing, and thus it was better that no names at all were given credit for the structure. Those interested in finding out the designers' names would eventually do so.

41. See Robin Cormack, *Writing in gold: Byzantine society and its icons* (New York: Oxford University Press, 1985).

42. Elizabeth Lipsmeyer, "The donor and his church model in medieval art from early Christian times to the late Romanesque period," Ph.D. diss., Rutgers University, 1981. They are represented, either in portrait medallions or coats of arms and insignia, on many other buildings as well, such as hospitals and town halls. See, for example, Evelyn S. Welch, *Art and authority in Renaissance Milan* (New Haven: Yale University Press, 1995).

43. See Donald Martin Reynolds, *The architecture of New York City: Histories and views of important structures, sites, and symbols* (New York: Collier, 1984), 176–178, for a discussion of the lobby corbels by Thomas R. Johnston of Gilbert, Woolworth, and others involved in the building's construction, as well as a summation of Gilbert's complex lobby decorative scheme.

44. Paul R. Baker, *Richard Morris Hunt* (Cambridge: MIT Press, 1980), 279–281.

45. The architect was John Wade. The mural, one of a number by Dodge, was entitled *Construction* and portrayed Wade putting the finishing touches on a model of the larger building. See John H. Conlin, *Buffalo City Hall:*

Americanesque masterpiece (Buffalo: Landmark Society of the Niagara Frontier, 1993), 26–27.

46. John Clubbe, *Cincinnati observed: Architecture and history* (Columbus: Ohio State University Press, 1992), describes, for example, several buildings that follow this convention. The Cincinnati Stock Exchange of 1921 supposedly contains faces caricaturing the building's architects and their attorney (123). Cincinnati's Union Terminal, opened not many years later, contains mosaic portraits of a whole string of officials, including the city manager, the terminal president, the mayor, and the supervising engineer. In England, carved corbels in the Rochdale Town Hall immortalized both the mayor and the architect. See Colin Cunningham, *Victorian and Edwardian town halls* (London: Routledge and Kegan Paul, 1981), 198.

47. For one such note the details on the recently completed museum building of the Wolfsonian Foundation for Decorative and Propaganda Arts in Miami Beach.

48. For more on souvenir building models see Margaret Majua and David Weingarten, *Souvenir building, miniature monuments: From the collection of Ace Architects* (New York: Abrams, 1996).

49. For one celebrity buildings and its souvenir reproduction see Philip Dennis Cate, ed., *The Eiffel Tower: A tour de force, its centennial exhibition* (New York: Grolier Club, 1989). Civic and commercial boosterism also played a role in stimulating the creation of presentation silver re-creations of building projects. See Katherine S. Howe, "In honor of the conspicuous consumer: Tiffany & Co. presentation silver," *Journal of Decorative and Propaganda Arts* 9 (Summer 1988), 60–67.

50. There was, of course, an old tradition of depicting buildings on medals of various kinds. See, for example, R. C. Bell, *The building medalets of Kempson and Skidmore* (Newcastle: Frank Graham, 1978), the fifth of a six-volume work dealing with token coinage issued during the reign of George III. Theatres, bridges, government buildings, libraries, and breweries were among the buildings depicted.

51. For ninety years of Flatiron photographs see Peter Gwillim Kreitler, *Flatiron: A photographic history of the world's first steel frame skyscraper, 1901–1990* (Washington: American Institute of Architects Press, 1990).

52. For picture postcards in general see George and Dorothy Miller, *Picture postcards in the United States, 1893–1918* (New York: Crown, 1976); and Martin Willoughby, *A history of postcards: A pictorial record from the turn of the century to the present day* (London: Studio Editions, 1992).

53. For more on the role of postcards and photographs in creating urban imagery see M. Christine Boyer, *The city of collective memory: Its historical imagery and architectural entertainments* (Cambridge: MIT Press, 1994), chap. 6. The history of architectural photography as such is examined by Robert Elwall, *Photography takes command: The camera and British architecture, 1840–1939* (London: RIBA Heinz Gallery, 1994); Robert A. Sobieszek, *The architectural photography of Hedrich-Blessing* (New York: Holt, Rinehart, and Winston, 1984); and *Architectural photography and the growth of the cities, 1850–1914* (Stuttgart, 1988).

54. Pierre Proveyeur and June Hargrove, *Liberty: The French-American statue in art and history* (New York: Harper and Row, 1986).

55. General Duncan S. Walker, ed., *Celebration of the one hundredth anniversary of the laying of the corner stone of the capitol of the United States* (Washington: Government Printing Office, 1893).

56. See the complex of events held to mark the one hundredth birthday of the (still uncompleted) Cathedral of St. John the Divine in New York City. Ian Fisher, "Cathedral marks century," *New York*

Times, Dec. 28, 1992. And, like human centenarians getting Willard Scott's morning greetings, hundred-year-old buildings are obtaining their own respectful recognition. See M. W. Newman, "The 100 Year Club," *Chicago Tribune,* Sept. 10, 1997.

57. See Ian Ousby, *The Englishman's England: Taste, travel, and the rise of tourism* (Cambridge: Cambridge University Press, 1990), chap. 1.

58. See Adrian Tinniswood, *A history of country house visiting: Five centuries of tourism and taste* (Oxford: Blackwell and the National Trust, 1989), for the details that follow.

59. For more on the rise of organized tourism see Piers Brendon, *Thomas Cook: 150 years of popular tourism* (London: Secker and Warburg, 1991). For the United States see John A. Jakle, *The tourist: Travel in twentieth-century North America* (Lincoln: University of Nebraska Press, 1985); and Dona Brown, *Inventing New England: Regional tourism in the nineteenth century* (Washington: Smithsonian Institution Press, 1995).

60. *USA plant visits, 1977–1978* (Washington: Government Printing Office, 1978), suggests the huge number of plant tours available today. Hundreds of industrial tours are included, among them bakeries, automobile factories, newspapers, wineries, and textile mills. While not primarily architectural in character, many tours must inevitably concern themselves with the buildings as well as the processes they house. For comments on the early-twentieth-century factory tour see David E. Nye, *American technological sublime* (Cambridge: MIT Press, 1994), 127–133.

61. For some references to this literature see Neil Harris, "Urban tourism and the commercial city," in William R. Taylor, ed., *Inventing Times Square: Commerce and culture at the crossroads of the world* (New York: Russell Sage, 1991), 66–82.

62. For the history of tourism in America see Earl Pomeroy, *In search of the golden West: The tourist in western America* (New York: Knopf, 1957); John F. Sears, *Sacred places: American tourist attractions in the nineteenth century* (New York: Oxford University Press, 1989); and John A. Jakle, *The tourist: Travel in twentieth-century North America* (Lincoln: University of Nebraska Press, 1985).

63. The opposition of many reformers to commercial display is studied in many essays by William H. Wilson and summarized in his broad survey *The City Beautiful movement* (Baltimore: Johns Hopkins University Press, 1989).

64. Joseph Rykwert, *The idea of a town: The anthropology of urban form in Rome, Italy, and the ancient world* (Princeton: Princeton University Press, 1976), 137.

65. For more on concierges see Jean-Louis Deaucourt, *Première loges: Paris et ses concierges au XIXe siècle* (Paris: Aubier Collection historique, 1992). The position was apparently invented sometime between 1820 and 1840 and was seized upon by a whole series of French literary figures, including Balzac and Eugène Sue, as well as by contemporary caricaturists.

66. These figures are taken from United States Bureau of the Census, *Special report: Occupations at the 12th census* (Washington: United States Printing Office, 1904).

67. Elwood P. Cubberley, *The principal and his school: The organization, administration, and supervision of instruction in an elementary school* (Boston: Houghton Mifflin, [1923]), 209.

68. For more on the evolution of building codes see Roger H. Harper, *Victorian building regulations: Summary tables of the principal English building acts and model by-laws, 1840–1914* (London: Mansell, 1985); Clifford Cyril Knowles, *The history of building regulation in London, 1189–1972* (London: Architectural Press, 1972); John P. Comer, *New York City building control, 1800–1941* (New York: Columbia University Press, 1942); and *A history of*

real estate, building, and architecture in New York City during the last quarter of a century (New York: Real Estate Record Association, 1898). This last was reprinted by Arno in 1967.

69. One example among many of the profits janitors supposedly realized can be found in a humorous anecdote, "He lost a snap," *Life* 22 (Sept. 28, 1893), 202. A cantankerous and virulently anti-Irish visitor from England observed that "American apart-houses are managed by a fierce sort of creature, barely human, who is known as the janitor. This animal lives in a sort of cave, waved in among the coal cellars. He never emerges except to swear or create a disturbance. He has absolute power of life and death over the trembling tenants." Montague Vernon Ponsonby, *The preposterous Yankee* (London: Limpus, Baker, 1903), 4–5.

70. "Janitors and apartment houses," *New York Times*, Mar. 28, 1905.

71. Charles Everand Reeves, "An analysis of janitor service in the elementary schools," Ph.D. diss., Teachers College, Columbia University, 1925. Controversies over the role of school custodians have continued to the present. For some recent New York City contractual disputes see Charisse Jones, "Pact eases New York school custodians' grip," *New York Times*, May 5, 1994; and Steven Lee Myers, "Giuliani wants better deal," *New York Times*, May 6, 1994.

72. The builders themselves were organized earlier. For Chicago see Chad Wallin, *The builder's story: An interpretive record of the Builders' Association of Chicago Inc.* (Chicago: Builders' Association of Chicago, 1966). For a fascinating commentary on maintenance, remodeling, and adaptive reuse, which I found after most of my project was completed, see Stewart Brand, *How buildings learn: What happens after they're built* (New York: Viking Penguin, 1994).

73. Earle Shultz and Walter Simmons, *Offices in the sky* (Indianapolis: Bobbs-Merrill, 1959), 89. This book devotes a chapter to "The building manager," 82–93, followed by another, "The building industry organizes," 94–105.

74. C. T. Coley, "Giving the tenants service in the Equitable Building," *Buildings and Building Management* 15 (May 1915), 27. This is part of a series of short interviews with figures involved with the construction of the Equitable.

75. Quite a few American cities experienced the growth of office-building maintenance. For one early-twentieth-century commentary see Carrie Westlake Whitney, *Kansas City, Missouri: Its history and its people, 1808–1908* (Chicago: Clarke, 1908), 506–510. Describing several newly constructed structures, including the Long, Scarritt, and National Bank of Commerce buildings, Whitney expressed her astonishment at their cleaning forces. "One man does no other work than to polish the door knobs and other metal work.... There is another man who spends the day polishing woodwork" (508).

76. Coley, "Giving the tenants service," 28.

77. For elevator fears and safety see Cecil D. Elliott, *Technics and architecture: The development of materials and systems for buildings* (Cambridge: MIT Press, 1992), 352–355.

78. Census figures presenting these changes are reprinted in Angel Kwolek-Folland, *Engendering business: Men and women in the corporate office, 1870–1930* (Baltimore: Johns Hopkins University Press, 1994), 30. Kwolek-Folland, particularly in chapter 4, provides excellent discussions of the spatial consequences of this transformation. See also Lisa Fine, *The souls of the skyscraper: Female clerical workers in Chicago, 1870–1930* (Philadelphia: Temple University Press, 1990).

79. These changes were caught by J. Lincoln Steffens, "The modern business building," *Scribner's Magazine* 22 (July 1897), 37–61. In this essay, fifth in a

series on the conduct of great busi-
nesses, Steffens paid particular attention to the decline of the tyrannical janitor, "a peevish, useless hanger-on,
whose sole purpose was to grind as
much as he could out of his natural
prey, the creatures given him with the
building by his patron, the owner" (57).
The building manager, with his
efficiency orientation, had replaced him.

80. John Beverley Robinson, "The tall
office buildings of New York,"
Engineering Magazine 1 (May 1891), 194.

81. Coley, "Giving the tenants service," 28.

82. *Buildings and Building Management* 25
(April 1915), 65.

83. "The window washer's romance"
appeared in *Buildings and Building
Management* 25 (January 1915), as did
"A few pointers on sponges."

84. One classic in this genre was Henry
Blake Fuller, *The cliff-dwellers* (New York:
Harper, 1893), centered on the four
thousand residents of the eighteen-
story Clifton, a "large and rather hetero-
geneous" assemblage.

85. *Industrial Chicago: The building interests,*
(Chicago: Goodspeed, 1896), 2: 127.

86. For the relation between self-generated
electricity and building maintenance
see Garth L. Magnum, *The operating
engineers: The economic history of a trade
union* (Cambridge: Harvard University
Press, 1964).

87. Earl Lifshey, *The housewares story: A his-
tory of the American housewares industry*
(Chicago: National Housewares
Manufacturers Association, 1973), 89.

3. Saying Good-Bye

1. Adrian Tinniswood, *A history of country
house visiting: Five centuries of tourism and
taste* (Oxford: Blackwell and the National
Trust, 1989), is the best source for the
early history of architectural tourism. See
the discussion in Chapter 2.

2. Several significant histories have been
written on architectural preservation
movements in various countries and
attitudes toward older structures. For
the United States see the two volumes

by Charles B. Hosmer, Jr., *Presence of
the past: A history of the preservation
movement in the United States before
Williamsburg* (New York: Putnam,
[1965]); and *Preservation comes of age:
From Williamsburg to the National Trust,
1926–1949* (Charlottesville: National
Trust and the State University Press of
Virginia, 1981); as well as James
Marston Fitch, *Historic preservation:
Curatorial management of the built world*
(New York: McGraw-Hill, 1982). For
Great Britain see Roy Strong, *Lost treasures of Britain: Five centuries of creation
and destruction* (London: Viking, 1990),
particularly the final chapter, which
reviews the heritage movement from
the foundation of the National Trust in
1895 through the passage of the
National Heritage Act of 1980. The
Society for the Protection of Ancient
Buildings was formed in 1877, partly
through the impetus of William Morris.
Stephen William Jacobs, "Architectural
preservation: American development
and antecedents abroad," Ph.D. diss.,
Princeton University, 1966, contains a
comprehensive summary of preservation efforts abroad and at home, concentrating on the period since the eighteenth century. George Christos
Skarmeas, "An analysis of architectural
preservation theories: From 1790 to
1975," Ph.D. diss., University of
Pennsylvania, 1983, reviews conflicting
approaches to preservation and conser-
vation from the eighteenth century to
the recent past. The amount of legislation passed in the United States during
the past half-century is demonstrated in
Richard L. Tubesing, *Architectural
preservation in the United States,
1941–1975: A bibliography of federal, state,
and local government publications* (New
York: Garland, 1978). For an attempt to
link preservation sentiments with contemporaneous ideological needs see
James M. Lindgren, "'The rising
grandeur of a nation and the decay of
its virtue': Historic preservation at the
fin de siècle," in Jürgen Kleist and

Bruce A. Butterfield, eds., *Fin de siècle: 19th and 20th century comparisons and perspectives* (New York: Peter Lang, 1996). And for one recent local study see Theodore W. Hild, "The demolition of the Garrick Theater and the birth of the preservation movement in Chicago," *Illinois Historical Journal* 88 (Summer 1995), 79–100.

3. Barnet Phillips, "The construction of great buildings," *Harper's Weekly* 34 (Ap. 12, 1890), 292.

4. Strong points out that destruction and demolition of historic buildings, by accident as well as by intention, had a long history and that loss of an important structure did not, before our own era, invariably produce a desire to reproduce it. "Today . . . if anything is destroyed we timidly replace it with a facsimile." *Lost treasures of Britain*, 22.

5. One of the few surveys of this process is Spiro Kostof, "His majesty the pick: The aesthetics of demolition," *Design Quarterly* 118/119 (1982), 32–41. Concentrating on the twentieth century, Kostof also invokes the monumental plans of Napoleon and Haussmann.

6. For more on Haussmann's efforts see David H. Pinkney, *Napoleon III and the rebuilding of Paris* (Princeton: Princeton University Press, 1958).

7. For a brief discussion and some illustrations see Cervin Robinson and Joel Herschman, *Architecture transformed: A history of the photography of buildings from 1839 to the present* (New York: Architectural League of New York; Cambridge: MIT Press, 1987), 47–51.

8. For more on the impact of these events, although not necessarily from this perspective, see Judd Kahn, *Imperial San Francisco: Politics and planning in an American city, 1897–1906* (Lincoln: University of Nebraska Press, 1979); Ross Miller, *American apocalypse: The great fire and the myth of Chicago* (Chicago: University of Chicago Press, 1990); Carl S. Smith, *Urban disorder and the shape of belief: The Great Chicago Fire, the Haymarket bomb, and the model town of Pullman* (Chicago: University of Chicago Press, 1995).

9. The political strategies behind new statehouses (as well as old) are sketched briefly in Henry-Russell Hitchcock and William Seale, *Temples of democracy: The state capitols of the U.S.A.* (New York: Harcourt Brace Jovanovich, 1976). For one state's movement from old capitol to new see David Park Curry and Patricia Dawes Pierce, eds., *Monument: The Connecticut State Capitol* ([Hartford]: Old State House Association, 1979). For another project on an even grander scale see Neil B. Thompson, *Minnesota's state capitol: The art and politics of a public building* (St. Paul: Minnesota Historical Society, 1974).

10. For the decision to retain and restore the Michigan capitol see Kathryn B. Eckert, "Elijah would be proud: The restoration of the Michigan State Capitol," *Michigan History* 74 (July–August 1990), 16–19. For the kinds of physical details that endeared statehouses to popular audiences see, in the same issue, Kerry Chartkoff, "Unveiling a masterpiece: A walking tour through the restoration process," 21–28. For the preservation and remodeling of the California State Capitol at Sacramento, called at the time the largest preservation project undertaken in the Western Hemisphere, see the series of articles on preservation and remodeling in *Progressive Architecture* 60 (November 1979).

11. *Re-dedication of the Old State House, Boston, July 11, 1882*, 6th edition, (Boston: City Council, 1882, 1893), 117. Boston's enthusiasm may have been nurtured by the interest of some Chicagoans in transporting the structure to their own city, giving the residents a longer sense of history than their own young and fire-damaged past permitted.

12. See, among others, Earle A. Shultz, "The effect of obsolescence on the useful and profitable life of office buildings," National Association of Building

Owners and Managers, *Depreciation of office buildings: Its relation to income tax* (1925); and Earl A. Saliers, *Depreciation: Principles and applications* (New York: Ronald, 1923). Saliers's book, a later edition of a work first published in 1915, argues that the cost of wasting assets must be included in the calculation of production costs. Appendixes group buildings into four general classes, according to the materials used, and assign them varying average lives and depreciation rates. See 513–520.

13. Graham Aldis, "Modernizing old office buildings," *Architectural Forum* 52 (June 1930), 867–871.

14. Jensen is cited in Herbert Muschamp, "What makes a building shrivel up and die?" *New York Times,* Oct. 3, 1993.

15. For appropriate ceremonial recipes see John H. Fulweiler, "Behind successful grand openings," *Chain Store Age Executive* 54 (January 1978), 21.

16. It has origins and analogies, of course. There was considerable concern about the threats to health that dirty buildings presented, particularly school buildings, and about students' developing syndromes like "school fatigue." Some of this was noted in the discussion of school janitors in Chapter 2, but see, more particularly, the articles collected by Helen C. Putnam, *School janitors, mothers, and health* (Easton, Pa.: American Academy of Medicine Press, 1913).

17. See, for example, "Beware 'sick-building syndrome,'" *Newsweek* 105 (Jan. 7, 1985), 58–60; Ted Gregory, "Halting spread of sick structures," *Chicago Tribune,* June 27, 1993; and "DOT's main building found 'sick,'" *Washington Post,* Apr. 3, 1996.

18. Estimates by the federal government placed one-third of America's seventy million indoor workers at risk for exposure to poor air. See *Washington Post,* Apr. 3, 1996.

19. See, for example, Simon J. Bronner, *Piled higher and deeper: The folklore of campus life* (Little Rock: August House, 1990), 144–148; and Jan Harold

Brunvand, *Curses, broiled again! The hottest urban legends going* (New York: Norton, 1989), 253–358. Brunvand's text includes legends about shopping malls supposedly sinking into swamps, office buildings leaning out of course, buildings supposedly built back to front, architectural suicides, and similar matters.

20. John Handley, "History lessons earning 'A' in economics," *Chicago Tribune,* May 8, 1994.

21. See, among others, Sherban Cantacuzino, *Re/architecture: Old buildings/new uses* (New York: Abbeville, 1989); Barbara Diamonstein, *Buildings reborn: New uses, old places* (New York: Harper and Row, 1978); and Carl M. Highsmith, *America restored* (Washington: Preservation Press, National Trust for Historic Preservation, 1994).

22. Cantacuzino, *Re/architecture,* 8.

23. One such may have been a recent proposal to dismantle the seventeen-story Art Deco McGraw-Hill Building on Chicago's North Michigan Avenue and then reconstruct it around a newly designed set of interior spaces, all part of a complex agreement with commercial developers. See Nancy Ryan and Genevieve Buck, "A landmark compromise," *Chicago Tribune,* Feb. 6, 1997.

24. David Stevenson, *Sketch of the civil engineering of North America* (London: J. Weale, 1838).

25. Tom F. Peters, *Building the nineteenth century* (Cambridge: MIT Press, 1996), 255–257. Among other sources, Peters cites a Viennese journal's publishing, in 1844, a New York City house moving.

26. John Obed Curtis, *Moving historic buildings* (Washington: Department of the Interior, 1979). This move was made in 1899.

27. Richard J. Webster, *Philadelphia preserved: Catalog of the Historic American Buildings Survey* (Philadelphia: Temple University Press, 1976), xxv.

28. A group of extraordinary photographs and films testifies to the drama of the demolition itself. For one example see

the 1977 destruction of the Biltmore Hotel in Oklahoma City by Controlled Demolition, Inc., no. 174 in Cervin Robinson and Joel Herschman, *Architecture transformed: A history of the photography of buildings from 1839 to the present* (New York: Architectural League of New York; Cambridge: MIT Press, 1987).

29. Patricia Leigh Brown, "Would 'Las Vegas landmark' be an oxymoron?" *New York Times,* Oct. 7, 1993. Brown also discussed the subject of signage preservation and the effort to preserve our neon heritage.

30. A how-to literature of deconstruction has emerged, some of it appealing to the same delight in technical detail that manuals of construction service. See Jean Poindexter Colby, *Building wrecking* (New York: Hasting House, 1972). Colby claims to have published, in 1960, the first book describing the wrecking of a building, *Tear down to build up.* Hers is generally a positive spin on the taking down of structures. "Crash! goes the huge bucket through roofs and floors. Bang! goes the big iron ball against walls. Of course, these cranes are there for the presence of destruction.... However, in many ways they are a sign of progress, of the world moving forward to better housing." *Building wrecking,* 9.

31. See, among others, Stanley B. Burns, *Sleeping beauty: Memorial photography in America* (Altadena, Calif.: Twelvetrees, 1990); and Jay Ruby, *Secure the shadow: Death and photography in America* (Cambridge: MIT Press, 1995).

32. Paul R. Baker, *Stanny: The gilded life of Stanford White* (New York: Free Press, 1989), 155.

33. For Midway Gardens see Paul Kruty, "Pleasure garden on the Midway," *Chicago History* 16 (Fall–Winter 1987–1988), 4–27.

34. "The University of the City of New York," *Harper's Weekly* 38 (Feb. 24, 1894), 174.

35. Aldis, "Modernizing old office buildings," cites the youth of several Chicago office buildings, taken down to be replaced by others. These included the fifteen-story Champlain Building, which lasted twenty-one years, and the fourteen-story Trade Building, taken down at the age of fifteen.

36. The findings are discussed, and photographs analyzed, in Thomas F. Tallmadge, *The origin of the skyscraper: Report of the committee appointed by the trustees of the estate of Marshall Field for the examination of the structure of the Home Insurance Building* (Chicago: Alderbrink, 1939). The report, written in 1931, was published in the *Architectural Record* for August 1934, before being printed in pamphlet form.

37. Nickel's broader interests and concerns with architectural preservation are described in Richard Cahan, *They all fall down: Richard Nickel's struggle to save America's architecture* (Washington: Preservation Press, 1994). For an earlier episode, in which Nickel was also involved, see Theodore W. Hild, "The demolition of the Garrick Theater and the birth of the preservation movement in Chicago," *Illinois Historical Journal* 88 (Summer 1995), 79–100.

38. Julian Ralph, "Odd callings in New York," *Harper's Weekly* 32 (Oct. 19, 1889), 839.

39. Chicago House Wrecking Company, *Catalogue 145* (Chicago, 1906). The company paid $80,000 to dismantle the Chicago Fair and $450,000 for the privilege of razing the great St. Louis Exposition.

40. William E. Curtis, "Laying fair in ruins," *Chicago Record Herald,* June 14, 1905.

41. Boyden Sparkes, "Big-city buried treasure," *Saturday Evening Post* 198 (June 19, 1926), 46–48, 63 ff.

42. See "The Lipsett Brothers: Biggest wreckers in the building world," *Architectural Forum* 120 (January 1964), 76–77.

43. Edward N. Kaufman, "A history of the architectural museum: From Napoleon through Henry Ford," in Pauline Saliga,

ed., *Fragments of Chicago's past: The collection of architectural fragments at the
Art Institute of Chicago* (Chicago: Art
Institute of Chicago, 1990), 16–51. See
also Werner Szambien, *Le musée d'architecture* (Paris: Picard, 1988).

44. Michael Kammen, *Mystic chords of
memory: The transformation of tradition
in American culture* (New York: Knopf,
1991), part 3, contains an excellent
analysis of this phenomenon. The
1930s featured an even grander effort,
in both Britain and America, simply to
record the historic built landscape. The
Historic Sites Act of 1935 authorized
the National Park Survey to survey historic buildings, secure, preserve, and
make drawings, photographs, plans,
and so on. See Harley J. McKee,
*Recording historic buildings: The Historic
American Buildings survey* (Washington:
Government Printing Office, 1970).
Five years later, in Great Britain, the
National Buildings Record was estab-
lished. See *50 years of the National
Buildings Record, 1941–1991* (London:
Royal Commission on the Historical
Monuments of England, 1991).

45. See the description offered in Morrison
H. Heckscher, "Collecting period
rooms: Frank Lloyd Wright's Francis W.
Little House," in Thomas Hoving, ed.,
*The chase, the capture: Collecting at the
Metropolitan* (New York: Metropolitan
Museum of Art, 1975), 207–217.

46. Hugh Howard, *The preservationist's
progress: Architectural adventures in con-
serving yesterday's houses* (New York:
Farrar, Straus and Giroux, 1991),
164–165.

47. Patricia Leigh Brown, "Saving Gus's
home," *New York Times*, Jan. 25, 1996.

48. Patrick Geary, "Sacred commodities:
The circulation of medieval relics," in
Arjun Appadurai, ed., *The social life of
things: Commodities in cultural perspec-
tive* (Cambridge: Cambridge University
Press, 1986), 177.

49. Some, like a vice president of the
National Federation of Demolition
Contractors in Britain, even argue that

"a designer should be made to file his
specifications not only for the construction of a building, but also for its demolition." David M. Pledger, *A complete
guide to demolition* (Lancaster:
Construction Press, 1977).

50. One might note, although it is surrounded by museum walls, the presence of the Frieda Schiff Warburg
Memorial Sculpture Garden, established at the Brooklyn Museum in the
1960s, for "fragmentary landmarks"
from destroyed buildings, which serve
as mementos of the city's past. See Clay
Lancaster, Introduction to Stephen M.
Jacoby, *Architectural sculpture in New
York City* (New York: Dover, 1975).

51. Rick Hampson, "So what do you do
with an obsolete skyscraper?" *Chicago
Tribune*, Jan. 24, 1993. More recently, in
1996 and 1997, a whole series of skyscrapers in New York and Chicago have
been planned for conversion from
office to hotel or apartment use. See, for
example, Tracie Rozhon, "A scalloped
magnificence, a hotelier's earnest
dream," *New York Times*, July 24, 1997;
and J. Linn Allen, "Spurned office
building to become glitzy hotel,"
Chicago Tribune, July 12, 1997.

52. Camilo José Vergara, *The new American
ghetto* (New Brunswick: Rutgers
University Press, 1995), 219–220.
When he presented his plan to a group
of Detroiters, the "response was not
encouraging," Vergara noted wryly,
220–221.

53. All this is taken from a remarkable
address by Alfred Seelye Roe, commemorating the centennial of the cornerstone of the Massachusetts State House.
See *Centennial of the Bulfinch state house:
Exercises before the Massachusetts legislature, Jan 11, 1898* (Boston: Wright and
Potter, 1898), 19–20.

54. The literature of analysis and description for the Columbian Exposition is
enormous, but for these purposes some
broad texts like Stanley Appelbaum, *The
Chicago World's Fair of 1893: A photographic record* (New York: Dover, 1980);

and Reid Badger, *The Great American fair: The World's Columbian Exposition and American culture* (Chicago: Nelson Hall, 1979), might be sufficient.

55. John E. Ziolkowski, *Classical influence on the public architecture of Washington and Paris: A comparison of two capital cities* (New York: Peter Lang, 1988), 111–112.

56. Marian Card Donnelly, *The New England meeting houses of the seventeenth century* (Middletown, Conn.: Wesleyan University Press, 1968), 66–67.

57. See the paragraph of discussion and references in Jack Quinan, *Frank Lloyd Wright's Larkin Building: Myth and fact* (New York: Architectural History Foundation, 1987), 128.

58. During the nostalgia-ridden late Victorian era there were quite a few anticipations of the new genre in Britain and America, like Edwin Beresford Chancellor, *Lost London, being a description of landmarks which have disappeared, pictured by J. Crowther circa 1879–87 and described by E. Beresford Chancellor* (London: Constable and Houghton Mifflin, 1926), or the delight in contrasts as evidenced by the two E. C. Peixotto renderings featuring New York in 1800 and 1900, reproduced in *Harper's Weekly* 44 (Dec. 29, 1900), 1258–1259. There were also sporadic versions undertaken in the 1920s and 1930s, some of them from a professional perspective, like the evocatively titled John Mead Howells, *Lost examples of colonial architecture: Buildings that have disappeared or been so altered as to be denatured* (New York: W. Helburn, 1931). This volume had an introduction by Fiske Kimball, director of the Philadelphia Museum of Art, architect, and another campaigner for accurate record making of American colonial architecture. But for the most part the new literature of photographic comparison and recollection gets going in the United States during the 1970s. For important and insightful commentaries on nostalgia and preservation writ large, see the essays and books of David

Lowenthal, notably *The past is a foreign country* (Cambridge: Cambridge University Press, 1975), and *Possessed by the past: The heritage crusade and the spoils of history* (New York: Free Press, 1996); and Raphael Samuel, *Theatres of memory: Past and present in contemporary culture* (London: Verso, 1994), the first volume of a projected trilogy.

59. Constance M. Greiff, ed., *Lost America: From the Atlantic to the Mississippi* (Princeton: Pyne, 1971); Constance M. Greiff, ed., *Lost America: From the Mississippi to the Pacific* (Princeton: Pyne, 1972).

60. For the "lost" books see, in order of their publication, Nathan Silver, *Lost New York* (New York: Schocken, 1967, 1971); Hermione Hobhouse, *Lost London* (New York: Weathervane, 1971); David Lowe, *Lost Chicago* (Boston: Houghton Mifflin, 1975); James M. Goode, *Capital losses: A cultural history of Washington's destroyed buildings* (Washington: Smithsonian Institution Press, 1979); Mary Cable, *Lost New Orleans* (Boston: Houghton Mifflin, 1980); Jane Holtz Kay, *Lost Boston* (Boston: Houghton Mifflin, 1980); Larry Millett, *Lost Twin Cities* (St. Paul: Minnesota Historical Society, 1992); and Carleton Jones, *Lost Baltimore: A portfolio of vanished buildings* (Baltimore: Johns Hopkins University Press, 1993). For the "then and now" texts see, among others, here in alphabetical order by author, Paul Dorpat, *Seattle now and then* (Seattle: Paul Dorpat, 1984); Merrill Hesch and Richard Piper, *Ithaca then and now* (Ithaca: McBooks, 1983); Charles S. Kelly, *Washington, D.C., then and now* (New York: Dover, 1984); and Edward B. Watson and Edmund V. Gillon, Jr., *New York then and now* (New York: Dover, 1976).

61. "Only those who are unwavering in their nostalgic commitment to the past would claim that downtown Pittsburgh today, with its mix of elegant old and stylish new buildings, is not a far more pleasant and visually satisfying Golden

Triangle than existed fifty years ago."
Arthur G. Smith, *Pittsburgh then and
now* (Pittsburgh: University of
Pittsburgh Press, 1990), viii.

62. Hesch and Piper, *Ithaca then and now,* 7.

63. This is, of course, an immense literature, and includes a number of extraordinary texts. Among the massive efforts
of recent years one might point to Joe
Friedman, *Spencer House: Chronicle of a
great London mansion* (London:
Zwemmer, 1993); Sally Jeffery, *The
Mansion House* (London: Phillimore,
1993); Nicolai Rubinstein, *The Palazzo
Vecchio, 1298–1532: Government, architecture, and imagery in the Civic Palace of
the Florentine Republic* (New York:
Oxford University Press, 1995); Yolande
Oostens-Wittamer, *Victor Horta: L' Hotel
Solvay* (Louvain-la-Neuve: Institut
superieur d'archéologie et d'histoire de
l'art, College Erasme, 1980).

64. Quinan, *Frank Lloyd Wright's Larkin
Building;* Joseph Siry, *Carson Pirie Scott:
Louis Sullivan and the Chicago depart-
ment store* (Chicago: University of
Chicago Press, 1988); Joseph Siry, *Unity
Temple: Frank Lloyd Wright and architec-
ture for liberal religion* (New York:
Cambridge University Press, 1996).
Other building biographies, some of
them created from a more general view-
point, include John Tauranac, *Empire

State Building: The making of a landmark*
(New York: Scribner, 1995); Kenneth
Hafertepe, *America's castle: The evolution
of the Smithsonian Building and its insti-
tution, 1840–1878* (Washington:
Smithsonian Institution Press, 1984);
John Physick, *The Victoria and Albert
Museum: The history of its building*
(London: Victoria and Albert Museum,
1982). And there are still more popular
biographical forms, some of them pro-
motional or commemorative. See,
among many others, James Klain and
Arnold J. Band, *Royce Hall* (Los Angeles:
University of California at Los Angeles
Press, 1985); and Joe Sherman, *A thou-
sand voices: The story of Nashville's Union
Station* (Nashville: Rutledge Hill, 1987).

65. For a fascinating set of comments on
buildings as events see Herbert
Muschamp, "What makes a building
shrivel up and die?" *New York Times,*
Oct. 3, 1993.

66. Marshall Sahlins, "Goodbye to *tristes
tropes:* Ethnography in the context of
modern world history," *Journal of Modern
History* 65 (March 1993), 24–25.

67. See, among many others, Manfredo
Tafuri, *The sphere and the labyrinth:
Avant-gardes and architecture from
Piranesi to the 1970s* (Cambridge: MIT
Press, 1987).

Index

Page numbers in **boldface** indicate
   illustrations

Photo Credits

6 From Daniel W. Pfaff, *Joseph Pulitzer II
and the Post-Dispatch* (State College, Penn.,
1991), fig. 1   **8** Scala / Art Resource,
New York   **9** Erich Lessing / Art
Resource, New York   **10***t* Maurice
Babey, Basel / Joseph Ziolo, Paris
10*b* V & A Picture Library   **16** Yale Slides and Photograph Collection
20 Museum of Our National Heritage,
photography by John M. Miller
21*t* The Metropolitan Museum of Art. All
rights reserved.   **21***b* Department of
Special Collections, The University of
Chicago Library   **24***t&b* From Philippe
Rive et al., *La Sorbonne et sa reconstruction*
(Paris, 1987), 146, 147   **23** Giraudon /
Art Resource, New York   **28***b* Archives
of The New York Public Library, Astor,
Lenox, and Tilden Foundations
34*t* London Borough of Hackney, Hackney
Archives Department   **34***b* London
Borough of Newham   **35** From Robert
Bruegmann, *Holabird & Root: An Illustrated
Catalog of Works* (1991), vol. 1
37*t&b* The Library Company of
Philadelphia   **39***b* Collection of Neil
Harris   **41***t&b* Courtesy of The B & O
Railroad Museum, Inc.
42 The Andrew J. Russell Collection,
Courtesy of the Oakland Museum of
California   **43***t&b* Golden Gate Bridge
Highway and Transportation District
44 Library of Congress, Washingtoniana
Collection LC-USZ 62-51402
45*t* From Otto Mayr et al., *The Deutsches

Museum (London, 1990), 31
45*b* Courtesy John W. Reps
47 Page III-66, lower left; vol. III of
photographs documenting the World's
Columbian Exposition; c. 1894; platinum
print; neg. E20891. Photograph © 1997,
The Art Institute of Chicago. All rights
reserved.   **48** Page III-65, lower right;
vol. III of photographs documenting the
World's Columbian Exposition; c. 1894;
platinum print; neg. E20889. Photograph
© 1997, The Art Institute of Chicago. All
rights reserved.   **51***l* National Trust
Photo Library / Andreas Von Einsieder
51*r* From *Zeitschrift fur Innen-Dekoration*,
vol. 13, January 1902, 302–303
52 Buffalo and Erie County Historical
Society   **53** From Vincent F. Kubly, *The
Louisiana Capitol, Its Art and Architecture*,
© 1977 by Pelican Publishing Company,
used by permission of the licensor
55 Photograph by Neil Harris   **58** New
York Times Pictures / NYT Permissions
60 Fishbein Collection, Department of
Special Collections, The University of
Chicago Library   **61** Geneseo Lodge
#214, Free and Accepted Order of Masons,
Geneseo, N.Y.   **63***b* From *The Second
Tour of Dr. Syntax, in Search of Consolation*
(London, 1820)   **65** From *The Public
Ledger Building* (Philadelphia, 1868)
66 Ryerson Library of The Art Institute of
Chicago   **71***t* Department of Special
Collections, The University of Chicago
Library   **72***t* Photo courtesy of the
Rockefeller Center Management
Corporation, New York   **72***b*
Department of Special Collections, The

University of Chicago Library
74*t* Ryerson Library of the Art Institute of
Chicago   **73***tr&l, b* Department of
Special Collections, The University of
Chicago Library   **74***b*, **75** Collection
Centre Canadien d'Architecture/Canadian
Centre for Architecture, Montreal
76*r*, **77***t&b* From O. F. Semsch, ed., *A
History of the Singer Building Construction,
Its Progress from Foundation to Flag Pole*
(New York, 1908)   **78***t* Collection
Centre Canadien d'Architecture/Canadian
Centre for Architecture, Montreal
78*b* By permission of the British Library,
ADD MS 18850 fl4v   **79** Page II-13; vol.
II of photographs documenting the
World's Columbian Exposition; c. 1894;
platinum print; neg. E22046. Photograph
© 1997, The Art Institute of Chicago. All
rights reserved.   **81***t* Gelatin silver
print, accession number P1986.24.7
81*b* Golden Gate Bridge Highway and
Transportation District   **82** © BPI
Communications, Inc.   **83***t Pencil
Points*, vol. 12, October 1931   **84** From
Vincent F. Kubly, *The Louisiana Capitol, Its
Art and Architecture*, © 1977 by Pelican
Publishing Company, used by permission
of the licensor   **86***tl* From *Discovering
Pittsburgh's Sculpture*, photographs by
Vernon Gay and text by Marilyn Evert,
© 1983 by University of Pittsburgh Press,
reprinted by permission
86*tr* Germanisches Nationalmuseum,
Nürnberg   **86***b* From Kenneth
Frampton, *Architecture and Urbanism*
(Tokyo, 1994), 110   **88***l* From *Flatiron:
A Photographic History of the World's First
Steel Skyscraper, 1901–1990* (Washington,
D.C., 1990), 31   **93** Reproduced by
kind permission of the Thomas Cook
Archives   **106** From O. F. Semsch, ed.,
*A History of the Singer Building Construction,
Its progress from Foundation to Flag Pole*
(New York, 1908)   **116** From Ben Hall,
*The Golden Age of the Movie Palace: The Best
Remaining Seats* (New York, 1961), 259
118 The Library Company of Philadelphia
121 From J. M. and Brian Chapman, *The
Life and Times of Baron Haussmann*
(London, 1957), opp. 182
123, 124 Courtesy of the Bostonian Society /

Old State House   **127, 128** From
Kenneth Kingsley Stowell, *Modernizing
Buildings for Profit* (New York, 1935)
129, 131 From Barbaralee Diamonstein,
Buildings Reborn: New Uses, Old Places (New
York, 1978), 214–215, 228–229
132*b* From *Brooklyn Daily Eagle*, March 1,
1923   **133** California Historical Society,
FN-12921   **134** From Richard F.
Pourade, *Gold in the Sun: The History of
San Diego* (San Diego, 1966)
136 From Larry Millet, *Lost Twin Cities* (St.
Paul, Minn., 1992)   **138** Collection of
Neil Harris   **139** Department of Special
Collections, The University of Chicago
142*t* Courtesy of the Richard Nickel
Committee, Chicago   **142***b* Chicago
Stock Exchange Trading Room,
reconstructed in the Art Institute of
Chicago, scagliola, gilded plaster, stained
glass, terracotta, wood, etc., 1893–1894
(demolished 1972). The reconstruction and
reinstallation of the Trading Room in 1974
was made possible through a grant from
the Walter E. Heller Foundation and its
president, Mrs. Edwin J. DeCosta, with
additional gifts from the City of Chicago,
Mrs. Eugene. Photograph © 1997, The Art
Institute of Chicago. All rights reserved.
145 From John Freeman, *London Revealed*
(London, 1993), 69   **146** Carnegie
Museum of Art, Pittsburgh; Museum
purchase, gift of the Drue Heinz
Foundation   **147** Clear and leaded glass in
oak frame, 1912, center panel: 88.9 x 109.2
cm; side panels: each 91.4 x 19.7 cm.
Restricted gift of Dr. and Mrs. Edwin J.
DeCosta and the Walter E. Heller
Foundation, 1986.88. Photograph © 1997,
The Art Institute of Chicago. All rights
reserved.   **148** Photograph © 1997,
The Art Institute of Chicago. All rights
reserved.   **150, 151** Photograph by Neil
Harris   **153***t* Page III-40; vol. III of
photographs documenting the World's
Columbian Exposition; c. 1894; platinum
print; neg. E20842. Photograph © 1997,
The Art Institute of Chicago. All rights
reserved.   **153***b* Page II-50; vol. II of
photographs documenting the World's
Columbian Exposition; c. 1894; platinum
print; neg. E22170. Photograph © 1997,